VOLUME 26

AVRO
VULCAN

By Kev Darling

PUBLISHERS AND WHOLESALERS

Copyright © 1999 Kev Darling

Published by
Specialty Press Publishers and Wholesalers
11605 Kost Dam Road
North Branch, MN 55056
United States of America
(612) 583-3239

Distributed in the UK and Europe by
Airlife Publishing Ltd.
101 Longden Road
Shrewsbury
SY3 9EB
England

ISBN 1-58007-023-X

Designed by Dennis R. Jenkins

Printed in the United States of America

<u>Front Cover:</u> *Once a 101 Sqdn stalwart Vulcan B2, XM575 turns over Lincoln Cathedral on its way home. On note is the Decca Doppler unit located behind the port wheelbay which replaced the earlier Green Satin unit. Unusual for a series 301 ECU machine, XM575 sports a counterpoise panel over each set of jet pipe tunnels. (BAe/Avro Heritage)*

<u>Back Cover (left):</u> *Airbrakes were rarely left in the open position when the aircraft was on the ground. Here XJ782 appears to be receiving maintenance to either the A or B drive motors. The small trolley attached in the vicinity of the port gear bay is a hydraulic test rig. (Mel James)*

<u>Back Cover (top right):</u> *Climbing finally into the sun is the last ever flying Vulcan B2, XH558, on its way to a well-earned retirement. The deflection of the flight controls on rotation is worthy of note. (BBA Collection)*

<u>Back Cover (bottom right):</u> *The Vulcan featured a very versatile engine starting system. Only one needed starting before the throttle was opened to 80%. If the reason was a scramble all the cross feed valves were opened and the remaining three ECUs could be spun up at the same time. (NATO AM)*

TABLE OF CONTENTS

THE AVRO VULCAN

WARBIRD**TECH**
S E R I E S

INTRODUCTION

AND ACKNOWLEDGEMENTS

Silence. The four dark shapes sit brooding on their concrete fingers. As if from nowhere two coaches appear. Twenty little green figures begin to bundle out. Splitting into groups of five, they race towards the waiting bombers. From out of their hidey-holes the ground crew step to meet them. A swift verbal exchange of hellos and the crews disappear inside. Anti-collision lights begin their dizzy spin. From under once quiet wings comes the growing roar of four APUs shrieking into life. A cacophony of whines join in as the PFCUs come on line. The ladder is bedded down, the entrance door closes. Standing by the nose leg the crewchiefs signal the back chocks away. Passing through moves long practised a myriad times before, the two "lineys" obey before moving to the power leads. Signals are given, the leads are pulled clear, the door snaps shut. Then they wait. Over the land lines so that only those that need to know comes the command, "This is the Bomber Controller – readiness state zero two."

As if by the wave of a wand, a strange howling noise blasts its way from the underbellies of the mighty bombers as the rapid air start system smashes compressed air over the blades of the engine starters at 100,000 rpm. Slowly the very ground and air begins to shake as sixteen Olympus engines rumble majestically into life. The final chocks are pulled clear.

One more command passes over the wires, "This is the Bomber Controller

'V' force Alpha – scramble, scramble, scramble." Even as the final word dies, mighty spears of exhaust smoke blast out from behind as the aircraft roll forward. The ground crew run for cover. Like clockwork mice one after another the delta shapes hurtle down the runway. Rotate. Gear up. Gone. Silence.

To many in the watching crowd, be they General or layman, a four Vulcan scramble is a wondrous thing to behold. Dramatic perhaps, yet the Vulcan in all its guises has intrigued the professional and public alike. Even starring in a major film alongside an actor called Sean Connery has become one of their achievements. These events are now the stuff of history as the Vulcan flies no more although a round dozen complete examples still exist in the UK, the RAF detachment at Goose Bay Canada still cares for one whilst three are resident in the United States.

Of the foregoing preserved aircraft, at least two are taxied regularly and have support pages on the Internet should you wish further information. However these retired theatrics once hid a greater and deeper purpose as this slim volume attempts to show.

In compiling this account, I have been privileged to call upon the help of many ex-colleagues and friends who have delved deep

into their memories and photo collections to assist. Therefore I would like to thank Avro Heritage at Woodford and spokesman George Jenks for the factory shots and many useful snippets, Bob Archer for his unending help and enthusiasm, Christian Brydges at the NATO Air Museum for outstanding help in locating lost schematics, the boys at HSA Bitteswell, Damien Burke for providing close up photos at short notice, Ray Deacon and Bob Mitchell for providing hard to find photos, John Nickolls for sharing his photos and memories of Akrotiri all the way from New Zealand, Peter Russell-Smith for letting me rummage through his extensive photo archive yet again and last, but not least, a special mention to the man who was once my boss but has always been a friend – Mel James. Tribute must also be paid to all those at Specialty Press especially Dave Arnold and David Wright and my good friend Dennis R. Jenkins who got me into this in the first place!! Enjoy.

Kev Darling
1999

Vulcan B.2 XH534 climbs out after a roller landing. (C. P. Russell-Smith Collection)

BUILDING A DETERRENT

The evolution of Britain's independent nuclear deterrent begins prior to those dark days of World War Two when such weapons and their development were being postulated throughout the scientific world. This led in Britain to the forming of the ad hoc Maud Committee to collate and investigate the knowledge then available. In turn this led to a report being released in 1941 which stated, somewhat over optimistically, that the creation of an effective Uranium based weapon could be achieved by 1943 at an estimated cost of £5 million. Although these estimates proved a trifle askew, the committee's comprehension of such a bomb's effectiveness proved spot on. Their propounded theory stated that such a weapon could bring to bear the concentrated blast of 18,000 lbs. of TNT and would create massive amounts of radioactive material. Unfortunately, these precepts were to be proved more than right four years later.

With Britain embroiled in the throes of a European war, resources were not readily available to continue such research, thus it was decided that the Maud Committee members would contact their counterparts in America.

Warfare, it is said, advances technology at a sometimes alarming rate. However in peaceful America, research into atomic weapons was many years behind that of the British. Obviously the arrival of the British party and their persuasive arguments bore fruit as the US Government, by now utterly convinced, decided that development of such a weapon was, to quote "a good idea." Massive amounts of money and resources were soon allocated to the project with typical American passion. From this point the Manhattan Project came into being. The pinnacle of the work carried out during those desperate dark years finally culminated in two massive explosions which saw the Japanese cities of Hiroshima and Nagasaki virtually wiped off the map. Unfortunately, this particular development in warfare has proven to be one genie that cannot be shoved back into its bottle.

Known as the Washington in the RAF, the Boeing B-29 Superfortress was unable to carry the Blue Danube *weapon due to the geography of the airframe. This example is WF442 'KO-J' of 115 Sqdn. (C. P. Russell-Smith Collection)*

With the final surrender of Japan, the citizens of the Allied nations began to look forward to more peaceful and prosperous times. As if in celebration, the electorates of both Britain and America placed two new men in charge in both Downing Street and the White House, Premier Attlee and President Truman. With regard to nuclear policy, each was very inexperienced and Attlee was totally uninformed. Two such disparate Governmental setups inevitably led to friction between the 'haves' of the United States and the 'have nots' of Britain.

The premier tactical bomber in service with the RAF during the late 1940s and 1950s was the Avro Lincoln. Eventually replaced by the far more capable EE Co. Canberra, this piston-powered aircraft was dropped from the Blue Danube *programme at an early stage. (C. P. Russell-Smith Collection)*

Avro Lancaster PA474 represents the aircraft that was the backbone of Bomber Command for much of World War Two and the immediate period following. Although more than capable of carrying the weighty Blue Danube *weapon, its overall slowness and lack of manoeuverability quickly removed it from consideration as a carrier aircraft. (BBA Collection)*

Premier Attlee wrote many times to President Truman espousing the British case for the joint development of nuclear weapons although all was to prove in vain. By August 1946, the McMahon Act (better known as the Atomic Energy Act) had been passed by the U.S. Senate restricting the passage of information about nuclear weapon development.

Although the introduction of the Atomic Energy Act was supposed to restrict the control of information on the subject to one source, the decamping British team involved at Los Alamos had returned home with a large amount of knowledge. By now Britain was cut off from the expected flow of information that normally marked the special Anglo-US relationship and was faced with an expansionist Russia with designs on the rest of Europe. Britain's only choice was to develop a nuclear arsenal to protect herself and her allies. This in turn led to the creation of the Atomic Energy Research Establishment based at the ex-RAF airfield of Harwell in Oxfordshire. The brief of this organisation was simple and clear cut: to turn theory into practise in the creation of fissible material and the components required to deliver it as an effective weapon.

Although the Defence White Paper of 1946 spoke only of research and development, such were the political, social, and military pressures of the day that building such a weapon was inevitable. Not for the

pundits of that immediate postwar period were the cries of the anti-nuclear brigade. Their answer was that Britain should have the biggest and best that the nation could afford so that the circumstances that gave rise to Hitler and his regime could never occur again. Adding to this desire for her own nuclear weapons, Britain still had the urge to be seen as a world power especially as the Foreign Policy of the United States was very unclear at the time. A nuclear umbrella would be required and if America decided to revert to her prewar isolationist position again, then each country would be very much dependent upon its own resources.

However, the formation of NATO in 1947 changed all that. Even with NATO looming and the Western Union in place, continued development of atomic energy and weapons continued apace. Thus it was on 3 October 1952, that a nuclear device complete with all the trimmings was exploded aboard the frigate HMS *Plym* at the Monte Bello Islands test site. The effective detonation of *Hurricane*, the device's code name, spurred the design and development teams on to create and test the UK airborne deterrent weapon later code named *Blue Danube*.

To carry *Blue Danube*, a monster of a weapon at 10,000 lbs., would require an aircraft of reasonable size capable of traveling at a speed in excess of 500 kts. (575 mph), twice that of the aircraft available in the inventory of the RAF at the time. For the RAF, this would mean trading in the obsolete Avro Lancasters and its later development, the fast approaching obsolescent, Lincoln Mk.II. It was obvious from

The Short SA.4 Sperrin was the insurance aircraft for Spec.B35/46. Built under Spec.B14/46, only two were built before the production order was cancelled. This example, VX158, photographed in July 1955 had already been allocated to test duties, in this case for the Gyron Junior powerplant. (C. P. Russell-Smith Collection)

the outset that neither of these stalwarts was in reality capable of carrying out such a mission. Although both were capable of carrying the bomb load, the increase in Soviet preparedness in the areas of air defence and anti-aircraft defence would render both aircraft exceptionally vulnerable to destruction. Reluctantly therefore, Bomber Command came to the conclusion that the current bombers would remain committed to the night tactical bomber force. Even the temporary loan of over 90 Boeing B-29s thinly disguised as Washington B.1s did not ease the situation, as this American stalwart could not carry the proposed weapon due to the geography of the airframe.

Thoughts then turned to the use of jet powered bombers as the delivery method. Although the early powerplants had been very shaky

in their infancy, continuing development had seen increases in reliability almost on a weekly basis. Use of jet engines in fighter aircraft had in the main proven successful and it was only a short step to translate the idea into a strategic bomber. Early powerplants were renowned fuel guzzlers especially at low level, thus the train of thought turned to the idea that missions would be better flown at high altitude and at the greatest possible speed. Both in theory would avoid anti-aircraft fire which was limited in accuracy to approximately 40,000 ft. Another area that would gain from such an altitude would be the fledgling fields of radar and navigational avionics where greater accuracy was forecast.

Such theories are all well and good, however Britain faced a great problem, this being a lapse of expertise in transonic and supersonic air-

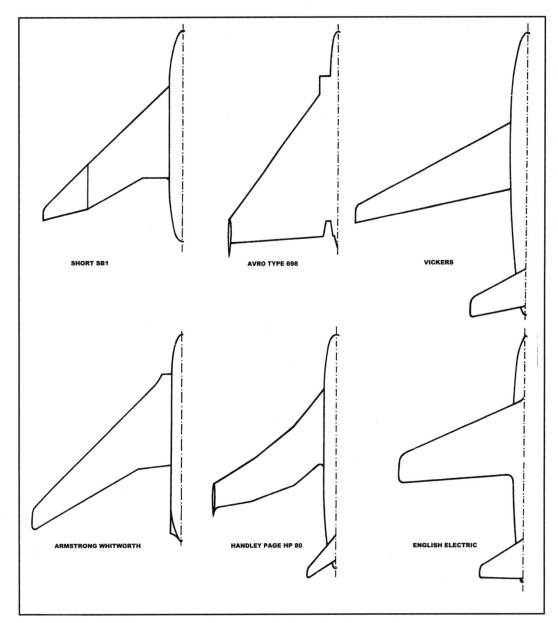

These basic diagrams represent the wing planforms submitted to the MoS in respect of Spec.B35/46 in May 1947. The successful entries were products of Avro, Handley Page, and Vickers with that of Shorts whose SB1 design evolved into the Sperrin. (BBA Collection)

SHORT SB1

AVRO TYPE 698

VICKERS

ARMSTRONG WHITWORTH

HANDLEY PAGE HP 80

ENGLISH ELECTRIC

frame design. Much of the theory of high speed flight was well-known, but the technologies and facilities to forward such knowledge were not. Undaunted, the war-battered aviation industry girded its loins and prepared to fight this new battle. First on the agenda was to develop the swept wing which was seen as a vital necessity in developing such an aircraft. The sweep was required to delay the onset of compressibility and boundary layer breakaway that had so dogged other efforts to puncture the transonic flight regime. With all of these

factors coalescing into one picture, a meeting of the Defence Policy Steering Group was held in 1947. This collection of experts postulated quite correctly that Soviet missiles and weaponry capable of destroying a high speed-high altitude attacker would not be on-line for at least ten years. Therefore the "Ten Year Rule" of development came into being.

By 1957, the UK had to have its share of the NATO nuclear deterrent, estimated at 200 weapons, in position plus the means of delivery. Rein-

forcement of the message came from the Air Ministry in early 1946 with the issue of OR229 to the aviation industry. This called for a Lancaster/Lincoln replacement powered by four jet engines. It had to be capable of delivering a 10,000 lbs. nuclear bomb at 500 kts. (575 mph) from an altitude of at least 45,000 ft. with a still air range of 3,500 miles. These latter figures were later revised upwards to 50,000 ft. and 5,000 miles respectively.

Having stated its requirements, the Air Ministry then passed the baton

onto the Ministry of Supply which in turn consulted the firms deemed most capable of turning the ideas into flying metal to see if it was at all feasible. Assured that such an aircraft could be designed and built the MoS restarted the paperwork trail again, this time for Spec. B.35/46 which was issued to selected firms on 1 January 1947. The refined set of requirements still called for the capability to carry a 10,000 lbs. bomb over 3,350 miles still air range in either day or night conditions from any base or camp anywhere in the world. The full range of available conventional weapons was to be available for the new bomber as was a reconnaissance capability. Further definition placed the all up weight at 100,000 lbs., as this was the limit imposed by the length and strength of the runways available. Further consultations with the Ministry by the manufacturers managed to gain a slight increase to 115,000 lbs. Height limits were set at 45,000 ft. achievable after one hour of flying with an increase to 50,000 ft. at the 2-1/2 hour point. Obviously it was hoped that the new bomber would gain further height advantages as more fuel was consumed. Cruising speed was set at 500 kts. (Mach 0.875) at continuous power over a target 1500 miles from base.

The rest of the specification was based on recent wartime experience although even here innovations were to the fore. Unlike previous bombers, a measure of manouverability over a great range of heights and speeds was deemed a necessity as was good provision for adequate warning and radio/radar countermeasures equipment. The tail end of the jet also came in for a sub part of the specification, in that the design should be capable of adopting a tail armament should other methods of defence prove unreliable or ineffective.

One of the most influential developments to emerge from World War II was radar. That chosen for the bomber spec based upon the very successful H2S system that first saw active service under the bellies of Lancaster and Halifax bombers. Such was its definition ability that it could pick out buildings from 20,000 ft. quite easily. To operate the new bomber a crew of five was settled upon. This consisted of two pilots, a pair of navigator/bombardiers, and a radio communications ECM operator. All were to be housed in a single pressure cabin that could be ejected as a single entity in the event of abandonment. One other proviso built into the specification was the requirement to build the chosen design at a rate of ten per month in the event of war using mass production techniques first pioneered in the earlier conflict.

Even though this specification was to take aeronautical engineering into new regimes of flight, aircraft design teams set to with a will creating the new bomber with enthusiasm. The MoS in the meantime had decided to restrict the competition to just six firms deemed capable of producing the goods. Thus on 9 January 1947, an invitation to tender for Spec.B35/46 was issued to Avro, Armstrong Whitworth, English Electric, Handley Page, Short Bros., and Vickers. After some months of frantic work, all six delivered impressive feasibility studies to the MoS during May 1947. It's all very well of course to ask for the future, but it is totally useless if you are presented with something that you do not fully understand. For a government department that had just grasped the piston-powered Lincoln to its chest, the futuristic concept it had initiated proved to be too much. In concert with the OR Branch and the Air Ministry, the decision was taken to pass everything onto RAE Farnborough for analysis.

Destined to be the first of the "V" Bombers to enter service, the Vickers Valiant was a slightly simpler design in comparison to the later Victor and Vulcan, although it did feature such novel innovations as electrically driven flaps and landing gear. (C. P. Russell-Smith Collection)

To collate all the available data, the Advanced Bomber Group was created and charged with defining the best from the six designs offered. Eventually the Avro Type 698 (later the Vulcan) and the Handley Page H.P.80 (later the Victor) were selected . The Avro design hinged on the use of a delta shaped wing whilst the H.P.80 featured a swept crescent shaped wing. As this was radical stuff, it was felt that an insurance policy aircraft would be required in the interim. Such an aircraft was to cover the basic idea of the original specification, but to a lower standard. This get out clause had been built into the original specification, and at the outset the RAF had decided to implement it. This was done so that when the definitive jet powered heavies entered service with Bomber Command, they would be greeted by personnel already familiar with the operating procedures required.

Activated under the alternative Spec B.14/46, known as the simple bomber project, this was allocated to Short Bros. of Belfast. They responded by building the SA.4. Throughout the period of 1948-51, the design and assembly work proceeded. On 10 August 1951, the first prototype, soon to be named Sperrin, flew for the first time. Even as the Short Bros. company was toasting success, moves were afoot to cancel the project. In essence it was quickly realised that the Sperrin was nothing more than a 1940s aerodynamic design with jet engines instead of piston. In the end, the Air Ministry finally settled upon one of the other contenders. To Vickers fell the plaudit of building the Valiant, the first of the "V" bombers into RAF service. Even though it was intended as a lower specification aircraft, it too featured many unusual innovations although that is another story entirely.

The development of the Avro Type 698 was progressing well even though politics, as per normal, had a habit of rearing its ugly head at the most inopportune moment to interfere with design policy. Even with these unneeded interruptions the programme was progressing logically and steadily enough for the MoS to issue an "instruction to proceed." With this written guarantee to cover the development costs, the Avro Type 698 project moved into high gear to bring to life that most famous of all the "V" bombers – the Avro Vulcan.

Avro's biggest rival was Handley Page whose prototype H.P.80 Victor, WB771, is pictured at Farnborough in September 1953. Of note is the careful smooth blending of all the constituent parts of the airframe. (C. P. Russell-Smith Collection)

FROM PAPER TO METAL

Although Avro had secured a contract to build one of the RAF's new bombers, the company understood quite clearly that a quantum leap was being made in technology and aerodynamics from earlier products such as the Lancaster and Lincoln.

The 1950s was an era of innovation and experimentation – no super computers here. An idea could be sketched, weight and balances played with, until a viable design emerged on paper. It fell to the Avro Project office to bear the initial responsibility for developing ideas. In this case, newly promoted Avro Technical Director, the designer Roy Chadwick, was involved in the roughing out of the Avro Type 698. However, much of his time was taken up in political manouvering in support of the project. Recalled by colleagues as a most innovative individual, he took to the new design and its inherent challenges with gusto, albeit from a distance.

Unfortunately for all concerned, this most famous designer of such stalwarts as the Lancaster bomber was never to see the Delta bomber fly that he supported so strongly. On 23 April 1947, the prototype Avro Tudor lifted off from the company airfield at Woodford. On board were Chadwick and his test

team. They were never to return as the aircraft rolled and crashed just after takeoff due to incorrectly assembled aileron controls. Although the death of such a great servant to the aviation industry shocked Avro, the company continued on the path.

One of the greatest problems facing designers using the delta shape and co-related flying wings is the issue of longitudinal stability. Initial design precepts had envisaged the Type 698 as a pure delta with everything encompassed within the airframe – very much the

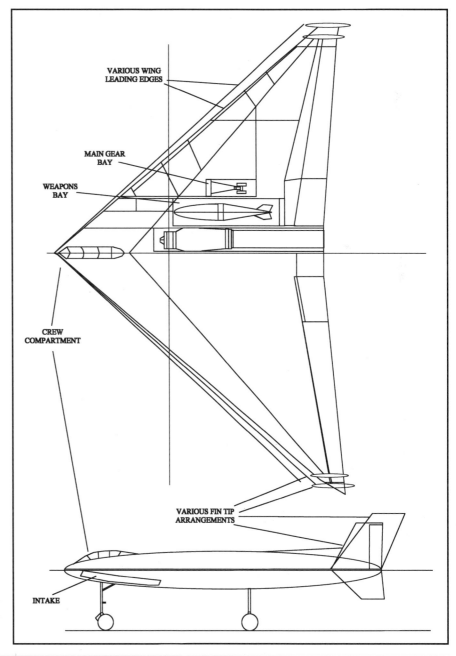

Resampled from a very blurry original, this diagram illustrates well the original flying wing concept proposed for the Vulcan. The original is said to be the work of Roy Chadwick. (BBA Collection)

VARIOUS WING
LEADING EDGES

MAIN GEAR
BAY

WEAPONS
BAY

CREW
COMPARTMENT

VARIOUS FIN TIP
ARRANGEMENTS

INTAKE

This photo of the Northrop YRB-49A represents well the problems facing designers trying to create the pure flying wing. It took the same company many years to finally achieve a workable vehicle in the shape of the revolutionary B-2 Spirit. (C. P. Russell-Smith Collection)

designer's utopian dream. Wing depth at the centre was calculated to be thick enough to contain the weapons bay, fuel tanks, engines, and crew compartment quite comfortably. The advantage of such a shape would also let the aerodynamics people add their requirements to the design with very little need for trade off as both disciplines could be accommodated quite easily. As the whole concept was revolutionary, it came as no surprise to find that the conventional fin and rudder had been traded off for the far more innovative idea of smaller versions mounted on the wing tips.

Although feedback and cross-pollination of ideas was noticeable by its absence between rival design teams, the experiences of the Northrop designed YB-49 Flying Wing plus data from the RAE Farnborough wind tunnel tests soon brought to light a problem. Unstable airflow patterns across the apex of the wing centre section would in turn nullify any advantages gained by the incorporated sweep back and cause problems with flight control effectiveness. To cure this problem a reduction in wing chord/thickness was proposed, which led to the emergence of a short front fuselage. A further step in the evolution chain saw the engines being placed side by side instead of adhering to the original plan to superimpose and feed the airflow through common pitot style intakes to the compressor faces. Another addition to the design, also intended to help stabilize the design, was a short rear fuselage located between the pairs of engine jet pipes. This move placed the bomb bay in its final position between the paired engines, an initial proposal to house the weapons payloads in under wing nacelles having been dropped.

Such a novel aerodynamic shape obviously required a novel flight control system. The development team at Avro proposed in April 1948 that control be exercised through all moving wing tips which would alter course by moving either in conjunction or differentially.

A few months later this idea had been dropped in favour of conventional ailerons and elevators all located on the wing's trailing edge. The all moving wing mounted fins were also dropped in favour of a conventional fin and rudder whilst the pitot intakes also changed shape to a more ovoid shape. Further wind tunnel testing showed that by now the design was shaping up to be more stable without any violent boundary layer breakaways occurring. With the fantastic now being developed into the usable, the proposal was given to the Avro Design Team to turn ideas into metal. Before that was to happen, however, both Avro and the MoS agreed that more research

work was required to verify the wing planform and the associated flight control systems. This led to the proposal to build flying scale models of the aircraft.

This programme, designated the Avro Type 707 series, was initially concentrated upon a Derwent powered mini delta which was to be used for low speed handling and evaluation trials. To explore the outer parts of the flight envelope, it was proposed to build the Avro Type 710 powered by a pair of Rolls Royce Avon turbojets. It was confidently predicted that this airframe would be able to explore the ultimate areas of the Type 698's regime, namely a maximum altitude of 60,000 feet and a top speed of Mach 0.95.

Further funding was also allocated for the construction of a basic full-size Type 698 to verify the design's suitability before the first full prototype was flown. Although the development concept looked good on paper, further scrutiny of the requirements and costs involved brought about a re-evaluation of the whole flight testing research phase. Another area that began to cause concern was the projected time scale to first flight of the first

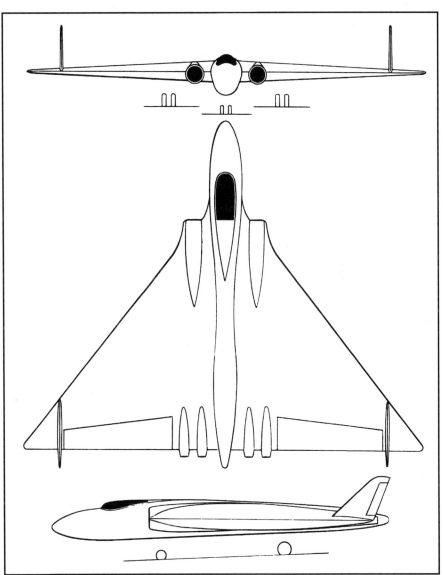

At this point some of the Type 698's salient features had appeared such as the forward fuselage although the pitot style intakes and wingtip fins were still in the equation. (BBA Collection)

proper prototype. These concerns resulted in meetings between Avro and the Ministry, and a production schedule was finally set for the test and development vehicles which led to the issuance of Spec E.15/48.

This specification saw the Avro Type 710 dropped from the programme altogether as an unnecessary waste of resources. At this point the programme consisted of a pair of low speed Avro 707 deltas flying with 1/3rd scale wings. Design and initial construction began in 1948 with first metal being cut late that year – the initial intention to build the wing of wood having been dropped as unrealistic. The first delta wing, a fairly simple two-piece design, was therefore placed in its jig in the early months of 1949. In order to keep costs down and speed up, the programme used readily-available components from outside sources.

From the Gloster Meteor came the nose gear and canopy and the main gears came from the Avro Athena trainer. The Derwent engine, also borrowed from the Meteor, was placed in the upper fuselage with the intake projecting above the top fuselage skin line. Although this form of intake is very inefficient, due to its location, it was deemed acceptable as the vehicle would be restricted to the low speed test range.

Construction continued apace at Avro's Woodford factory enabling the first 707, VX784, to be rolled out in August 1949. After the usual functional and taxi runs, it was dismantled and taken by road to the A&AEE at Boscombe Down arriving on 26 August. First flight of the research aircraft took place late in the evening of 4 September with no problems being reported. Encouraged by such success,

arrangements were made for this, Britain's first tailless delta, to appear at the 1949 SBAC Farnborough show in the static display line up.

Test flying during September showed that the delta shape differed little in performance at low speed from other aircraft except for the need for a slightly longer take-off run. Further flights took place, but were stopped on 30 September when the 707 crashed killing Test Pilot Eric Esler. Investigation into the crash showed there to have been a problem with the airbrake control circuit which had caused an unrecoverable low altitude stall.

With the basic premise of the design cleared of blame, work on the second Avro Type 707 was allowed to continue. By this time Avro had expressed a desire to include some improvements into this second vehicle. These included

This view of VX748 illustrates well the upper fuselage intake for the Derwent engine. The lack of ejection seat is also readily apparent. (C. P. Russell-Smith Collection)

Designated as the Avro 707B, VX790 first flew on 6 September 1950 and quickly replaced the lost VX 748 on the low speed handling programme. (BAe/Avro Heritage)

an injection seat and other details that included engine installation and flight control behaviour. This was duly formalised by the MoS as Spec E.10/49.

On 6 September 1950, the second Avro 707, designated as a "B" model, first flew at Woodford before proceeding by road to Farnborough for the 1950 SBAC show. Two of the most obvious changes incorporated into this second test aircraft were the appearance of a proper forward fuselage and an extended nose leg borrowed from the Hawker P.1052. With its slightly nose up attitude, VX790 presented its wing leading edge to the airflow differently from its predecessor which helped to shorten the length of runway required for the takeoff run. Determined to prove to the world at large that the delta design

was a viable proposition, Avro Chief Test Pilot Roly Falk put the little blue delta through a series of airborne gyrations showing the SBAC crowd the aircraft's superb handling characteristics. Conventional aircraft have a tendency to stall at 15 degrees, even at 30 degrees the little delta was still fully controllable. Further tweaks to the design saw a revised intake being fitted in February 1951 as a result of wind tunnel testing at the Rolls Royce facility at Hucknall. This revised intake increased the speed range available for test flying. One other point that the Avro 707 successfully proved was that by angling the jet pipe end caps slightly outwards and downwards, a smaller fin and rudder could be fitted in place of that originally envisaged.

Although both the Type 707s had

proved the basic delta concept, there were those within Avro who were pressing for the construction of another test aircraft. This one however would be more representative of the aircraft that the Type 698 had evolved into, and would thus provide more accurate data that the design team could draw upon. These concerns were noted then acted upon, which in turn led to a complete redesign of the Type 707. The new model was given the now defunct "A" designation which confused nearly everybody.

Compared to the two earlier aircraft, the 707A revealed the changes to the wings and intakes that were proposed for the full scale aircraft. Destined to be a realistic scale model of the new bomber, the new aircraft also incorporated for the first time scaled flight control surfaces. Some systems were however still missing from the test aircraft, these including cabin pressurisation and initially powered flight controls. The omission of the latter gave rise to problems with out of phase movements of the elevators which finally disappeared when PFCUs were installed. Having first flown on 14 July 1951, WD280 clocked up 92 flying hours before the power controls were fitted in May 1952. By this time the test programme was playing catch up with the development of the full size aircraft, although the trials had discovered one problem that required fixing. This was an inherent buzz that increased proportionally to height and speed. This brought forth the comment that if the original test schedule had been adhered to, the expensive leading edges fitted to the first production batch of aircraft would not have required replacing.

In hindsight, many commentators would view the Type 707 programme as a waste of both time and resources, however their ability to fly well gave necessary reassurance to those involved in the project from the government downwards. As this was an era of expanding technologies, it is understandable that those investing should see some successful results before extra funding is put forth. Further enthusiastic support was garnered when the Controller of Supplies(Air) Air Marshall Sir John Bootham flew the Avro 707 in September 1951. After the flight, the Air Marshall recommended that a group of RAF pilots be allowed to fly the test vehicles so that experience of handling tailless deltas could be gained.

Further research Type 707s were to be built by Avro, although these aircraft were intended more for flying outside the Type 698 programme in the field of pure aircraft research.

In 1952, the RAE ordered one for such a purpose plus a side by side seated conversion trainer later to be designated the Type 707C. All four of the extant deltas later went on to pure research duties after completion of the Vulcan development programme.

Running in parallel with the Avro delta research programme, development of the full-sized article continued apace. The first contract for two prototype 698s had been received in March 1949, and with the first flight of the first Type 707 taking place a few months later much of the finished vehicle seemed to be in place. As with all plans hiccups do occur. This one was courtesy of RAE Farnborough where much of the wind tunnel testing had been carried out. Tests at the establishment had revealed a serious discrepancy between the performance figures of the Avro team in Manchester and those

Pushing the concept slightly further the type 707C, WZ744, was a two seat aircraft. Now preserved in the Cosford Museum it was used for powered flight control development and conversion training. (C. P. Russell-Smith Collection)

Showing a strong family resemblance to its larger Vulcan B.1 sibling parked alongside is Avro 707A, WZ736, which clearly revealed the evolution of the type 698 in miniature. (C. P. Russell-Smith Collection)

obtained under test using scale models. Many of the figures at the Manchester office had been arrived at using reasoned deduction based upon available theory and had been assembled before the appearance of the definitive forward fuselage in the design. Those from Farnborough showed that the altered fuselage and extensively changed intakes introduced an increased compressibility drag rise factor which would occur on the constant section wing at much lower heights and speeds than first anticipated. Such an increase would in turn lead to a serious reduction in overall performance which would be unacceptable to the eventual purchaser – the RAF.

Obviously these shortcomings had to be dealt with, therefore meet-ings were held between the various parties to try to resolve the problem. It was at one of these get-togethers that Mr. Barry Haines, the resident expert in supercritical wing performance at the RAE, suggested that the original wing design be scrapped and completely redesigned. The most obvious change to the casual observer was that the wing section was now thickest close to the leading edge, a major change from the earlier position that had placed the thickest point close to the tapered wing centreline. Notwithstanding this setback, Avro placed maximum resources on the redesign in December 1949. Such was the skill and determination that the assigned draughting team had completed the task by May 1950. The redesign did bring a few added benefits in improved intake perfor-mance and growth space for future projected engine development.

As construction continued on the prototype, Avro received a contract from the MoS for 25 production Type 698 aircraft. However this too had a hidden sting as Handley Page, Avro's biggest rivals, by now building prototype HP.80, also received a contract for a similar number of production bombers. This put pressure on both organisations as both companies were sure that only one would succeed in securing the contract that would place their aircraft in volume squadron service. To capture the imagination of the public for PR purposes, extra effort was put into completing the first airframe as quickly as possible. Such was the success of this initiative that the first prototype, VX770, in a gleam-

ing white finish was rolled out for public view in early August 1952. On 30 August, Avro Chief Test Pilot, Roly Falk, lifted the Type 698 prototype from the Woodford runway for its maiden flight. Missing systems on this first flight included cabin pressurisation, a second pilot's seat and the wing fuel system. This first landmark flight lasted 35 minutes, but was not without its problems, fortunately both were minor in nature. Initially the most serious was a nose gear red that indicated that the leg was not properly locked up in its bay. That this was a false indication was confirmed by the pilots in the chase aircraft, a Type 707 and a Vampire, who confirmed that the airframe was clean. The other problem concerned the main gear rear leg fairings both of which were torn off on takeoff. The cause was later traced to wing flexure problems and the lack of structural strength in the fairings and their mounts. After a safe landing, the pilot confirmed that the Type 698 was easy to fly and very manouverable, forecasts that had been made during the flight testing of the Type 707s.

Two days later, VX770 was at A&AEE where a further three hours of test flying were undertaken before this new radical shape in the sky was shown to the public at the 1952 Farnborough SBAC show. All told the prototype made five appearances at Farnborough before returning to Avro for installation of some of the missing systems and modification work.

During October 1952, a name for the new bomber was finally decided upon by the Chief of the Air Staff, ACM Sir John Slessor, and the Air Council. After weeks of intense press speculation, the name Vulcan was chosen which continued the "V" theme already in operation with the Victor and Valiant. Depending on whose version of Norse mythology you read, Vulcan is either a misshapen God of War thrown out of heaven or the Hammer of the Gods.

With a choice of name finally settled, Avro returned to the more pressing business of updating the extant Type 698 Vulcan. The missing fuel system and pressurisation systems were installed as was the missing co-pilot's seat. Many pundits have previously propounded before that the second pilot's seat was shoehorned into the cockpit at the insistence of the RAF. This is known to be a misinterpretation of a remark by the company test pilot who had claimed that the aircraft could have been safely and easily flown by one man. Contemporary observers insist that the Vulcan was always intended for two-pilot operation. The reason for this being that no one in his right mind would place the safe operation of a multi-million pound bomber in the hands of a possibly inexperienced pilot or leave the aircraft and the rest of the crew to their fate should the only occupant of the pilot's seat become incapacitated.

Improvements were also made to the ergonomics of the pilots' panels at the insistence of the chief test pilot who also insisted that a fighter type stick be installed in preference to the old style steering yoke.

In its haste to get the first prototype into the air, Avro had been forced to install Rolls Royce Avon engines rated at 6,500 lbs. st. instead of the projected Bristol BE10 powerplants. Eventually to emerge as the RR Olympus and to find further fame as the powerplant for Concorde, the BE10 first underwent ground test runs at the company's Bristol, Patchway, plant on 6 May 1950. Two years later, prototype engines were being run at Woodford in a ground test rig installed in a Vulcan wing mock-up. Airborne testing of the engine was to culminate in the capturing of the

world altitude record by a Canberra powered by a pair of Olympus Mk.99s. Although this venture was a success, the production engines were not scheduled for installation in VX770 until later that year. As this would cause unacceptable delays to the testing schedule, it was decided to ground the prototype Vulcan after 32 flying hours to enable the installation of slightly higher powered engines, in the shape of Armstrong Siddeley Sapphire 6s, to be carried out. The increase in thrust was not excessive, the Sapphire running at a maximum of 7,500 lbs. st. each, but it was enough to push the flight envelope further.

Further intensive test flying to expand the performance flight envelope continued over the next 60 flying hours achieved in 57 flights. Obviously the Sapphire prototype could only go so far in proving the Vulcan's performance, thus it was with some relief to all con-

cerned that the second prototype, VX777, was rolled out in August 1953 powered by Olympus Mk.100 engines rated at 9,750 lbs. st. each. First flight of VX777 was undertaken on 3 September 1953 and yet again Avro products dominated the Farnborough skyline during the annual SBAC show less than a week later. Highlight of the flying was the flypast in formation of the two prototypes in company with the surviving Type 707 test aircraft.

At the conclusion of the Farnborough junket, the second prototype was transferred to A&AEE to continue with the flight test development programme. However delays were encountered almost immediately with the need to modify the engines and the fuel flow control system which was experiencing imbalance problems. Having balanced the fuel flow system and its controllers, test flying resumed only to be abruptly halted on 23 July 1954 when VX777 was damaged in

a heavy landing at Farnborough. The subsequent repair period allowed Avro to install uprated Olympus Mk.101 engines rated at 10,000 lbs. st., not far short of the production engine's rating of 11,000 lbs. st. During the same time frame, the opportunity was taken to install Olympus engines in VX770, thus in early 1955 both prototypes were in a position to explore the outer edges of the projected Vulcan flight envelope.

It was at this point that further problems were encountered with the wings' compressibility. As both aircraft were now capable of both high speed and high altitude, it was discovered that application of "g" in this part of the flight regime was causing a mild high frequency buffet. This condition occurs to some degree in most aircraft and is caused by the separation of the boundary layer air flow from the wing. In a worst case scenario, such a condition if allowed to continue

Touching down at Farnborough in 1953 the first prototype 698, VX770, displays many differences from the production aircraft. Of note are the lower surface outboard airbrakes which were later discarded as superfluous. The nose also deserves some attention as it was completely metal in construction without a radome and lacks a bomb aimer's blister. An extra pitot head is fitted at the extreme tip. (C. P. Russell-Smith Collection)

A unique and rare sighting of early production examples of the Vulcan Victor and Valiant flying in formation over Farnborough in September 1958. Close study will reveal how closely the contestants adhered to their original wing planform proposals. (C. P. Russell-Smith Collection)

can cause total structural failure to the wing. Avro however were more concerned that range, bombing run accuracy, and a reduction in manouvereability would result. Although such behaviour had been hinted at by the Type 707A's flight trials, the lower powered Vulcan prototypes had been unable to achieve anything like full flight parameters prior to the installation of the Olympus engines.

Avro presented a brave public face to the world despite having to deal with a report from A&AEE, Boscombe Down, which pulled no punches in highlighting the faults discovered in the behaviour of the Vulcan prototypes. Primary defects in the design were as follows:

Above Mach 0.86 the aircraft displayed a strong nose down tendency. This was later cured by the installation of auto-mach trimmers.

With an increase of speed above Mach 0.89 problems were encountered with pitch damping. This was later resolved by the installation of the pitch damping system.

The Mach number/buffet characteristics were unacceptable using the aircraft's current wing planform.

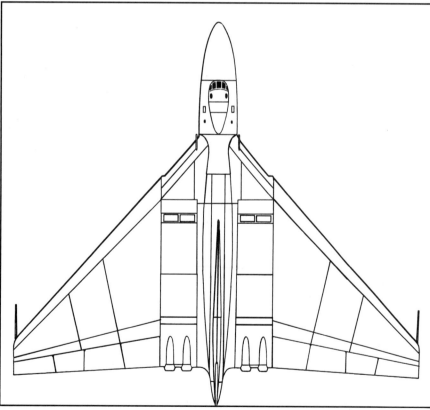

This is the first Vulcan wing planform that graced both prototypes and the early production Vulcan B.1s. (BBA Collection)

The final sentence however was the one that could have put paid to the Vulcan's RAF career as it ended thus "Although the aircraft has certain outstanding features serious deficiencies are present, particularly at and above the cruising Mach number range, and until these are rectified the Vulcan cannot be considered satisfactory for service use."

Realising that such a damming report could stop the project, a big meeting was called by the head of the design team, Mr. Stewart Davies, at Manchester to resolve the problem. All interested parties attended and eventually the solution was provided by the representative of the RAE Farnborough Hi-speed tunnel section. Later known as the Phase 2 wing, this required a new leading edge whose first section reduced the sweep from 52 degrees to 42 degrees, but was to return to it at the outer section. This cranking of the wing increased the outer chord by 20%. As well as rejigging the wing leading edge it

was also given a certain degree of downward droop. Accompanying the new wing shape were vortex generators placed ahead of the flight control surfaces to re-energise the boundary layer.

Although the problems of the Vulcan's handling and performance appeared to have been cured, the new fix arrived too late to be applied to the first production aircraft, XA889, which was rolled out at Woodford in January 1955. Major changes from the prototype aircraft included a fibreglass/Hycar nose radome to protect the H2S bombing radar and the installation of pre-production Olympus 101 engines, plus a slightly longer nose to contain the nose leg without the need for telescoping it. This latter modification also enabled an increased fuel load to be carried. First flight of the silver painted production machine took place on 4 February 1955 some twelve months ahead of the rival HP Victor. XA899 was eventually fitted with

the new wing leading edge in February 1958.

The improvement carried out to the Vulcan's leading edge must have been viewed as a success by those outside of the company as Avro later received another production contract to bring the final Vulcan B.1 total up to 45 aircraft on 30 September 1954. As for the prototypes, VX770 continued as a systems development aircraft with RR Conway engines until it was destroyed in a midair explosion over Syerston, Notts, on 20 September 1958 in which the crew were killed. The cause was subsequently traced to fatigue failure which caused fuel from the ruptured system to ignite. The second prototype, VX777, was later converted to serve as the Vulcan B.2 prototype and was first flown as such on 31 August 1957. It continued as an aerodynamic test vehicle during the period 1958-60. It was finally broken up at Farnborough in July 1963 after usage in runway braking experiments.

The second prototype 698, VX777, has streamed its TBC on landing. This view reveals quite clearly the location of the TBC bay door which was featured on all the Vulcan B.1s and the first production B.2s. (BAe/Avro Heritage)

Lifting off from Woodford, VX777 displays well the wing developed for the Vulcan B.2 known as the Phase 2C wing. (BAe/Avro Heritage)

Undergoing spares recovery prior to scrapping, VX777 sits at Farnborough in 1961. By this time the aircraft was close to that of the production standard Vulcan B.2. (C. P. Russell-Smith Collection)

ON TRIAL AND IN SERVICE

Having secured two production contracts for the Vulcan, Avro realised that to clear the aircraft for the rigours of everyday squadron service extensive testing would be required to iron out any problems that were likely to appear. It was also realised early on that as built the B.1 version was very much an interim as it lacked any credible form of self defence. However the solution to this particular lack initially took a back seat as the flow of production standard aircraft began.

As with many aircraft entering service from new, the provision of engines within the projected time scale can be a major stumbling block to completing deliveries. With the Olympus the Bristol Engines division of Rolls Royce seemed to have produced a winner, except for the odd hiccup the delivery of engines to each airframe ran smoothly.

This enabled the first two production bombers, XA889 and 890, to start the preservice trials programme where they were soon joined by the second prototype, VX777, which had received all the current modifications including production Olympus Mk.100 engines during the repair work incurred by its earlier heavy landing. Resuming test flying in January 1955, it was later upgraded to the final standard of B.1 engine – the Olympus Mk.101. Now just short of full production standard, the revamped aircraft was dispatched to Boscombe Down to investigate all aspects of engine handling including high altitude restarts, asymmetric flying, and engine out performance. Soon after this in mid 1955, the Vulcan was returned to Woodford where it was fitted with

First off the line – First production Vulcans XA889, XA890, and XA89 pictured at Chatterden being prepared for their first test flights. Under the wings these first few production aircraft still sported the outboard airbrake although this was soon deleted, the early Vulcans being modified retrospectively. (BAe/Avro Heritage)

a modified wing leading edge assembly, resuming test flying on 5 October 1955.

With the handling parameters now set for aircraft flying with the Phase 2 wing, VX777 was again returned to Woodford for further modification and this time the definitive auto-stabilisation system was installed. After the required plethora of ground checks and adjustments, test flying again resumed in December and was to last over six months and encompass 100 flying hours spread over 70 sorties.

Further airframes were also sent to the A&AEE to investigate and establish the Vulcan's handling and performance parameters. The first prototype, VX770, had already joined the Boscombe test fleet when the first production aircraft, XA889, arrived in March 1956. Having been involved with company test flying, the Vulcan had later been grounded for the instal-

lation of Olympus Mk.101 engines before proceeding. Both aircraft were now assigned to acceptance trials for the C(A). Initial service release clearance was granted on 29 May 1956. After the completion of these trials, XA889 was dispatched to Patchway, Bristol, where it was employed on the Olympus development programme. In March 1957, the first production Mk.102 engines rated at 12,000 lbs. st. were flown being swiftly followed in July by the first test flight of the Mk.104 rated at 13,400 lbs. st.

Radio and radar trials were to be the province of the second production Vulcan, XA890, which was allocated to the RAE soon after its appearance at the 1955 SBAC show. Destined never to receive the Phase 2 wing modification, the aircraft was also employed on ballistics research work at Farnborough before moving on to RAE Thurliegh, Bedfordshire, for blind landing experimental work with the BLEU.

Meanwhile XA891, the third production Vulcan, was also involved with trials work regarding fuel system performance, tank pressurisation, and operation of the nitrogen purging system to reduce the risk of fire and explosion due to vapour build up. Further production aircraft were also destined for trials work, thus XA892 became the armament trials machine whilst the next sequential pair were also involved for a short period. Dedicated auto-pilot system work was the province of the RAE Thurleigh allocated XA899. On 22 December 1959, whilst being operated by the BLEU, XA899 achieved a world's first by becoming the first four engined aircraft to complete a fully automatic hands off landing.

Although the RAF was eager to get its hands on its new aircraft, it was a great believer in the OCU system for introducing new aircraft to service. Thus it was to 230 OCU based at RAF Waddington, Lincolnshire,

The second production Vulcan never served with the RAF spending much of its working life with the RAE at Thurleigh, Beds being used by the BLEU. (C. P. Russell-Smith Collection)

This shot from above illustrates well the crank introduced into the wings leading edge under the Phase2 proposals. XA899 also spent much of its life with the RAE where it achieved the honour of being the first four jet aircraft to make an automatic landing. (BAe/Avro Heritage)

that the first production deliveries were made. Their first Vulcan was XA897 which arrived for acceptance on 20 July 1956. It was soon replaced by an earlier build aircraft, XA895, as the first bomber was returned to the Avro works at Woodford for modification. On 9 September 1956, XA897 departed the UK on a flag waving sales flight of Australia and New Zealand. In both countries the Vulcan showed that the resident air forces were suffering a serious lack of air defence assets capable of acting against such an aircraft. In the early hours of 1 October, XA897 depart-

ed from Aden on the last leg of its journey home to a VIP landing at Heathrow Airport. Due to a culmination of minor errors, the Vulcan touched down short of the runway which tore off its main undercarriage legs and left the aircraft uncontrollable. At 800 ft. AGL, the aircraft captain realising that a crash was imminent, called for the crew to abandon aircraft. He and the co-pilot, C-in-C Bomber Command Sir Harry Broadhurst, then ejected. Unfortunately the attitude of the Vulcan and its rapidly decreasing height left the rear crew of four, which included an Avro rep-

resentative, with no chance to escape and they were killed in the ensuing crash. Although no one person was deemed to be at fault, the subsequent inquiry and officialdoms' attempts to interfere left bitter memories in the minds of Bomber Command. One point that did emerge from this inquiry was the need to improve rear crew escape facilities. Although many schemes were put forward during the service life of the Vulcan, all were doomed to fail either through being impractical or the lack of political will to implement the required changes. Two of the more

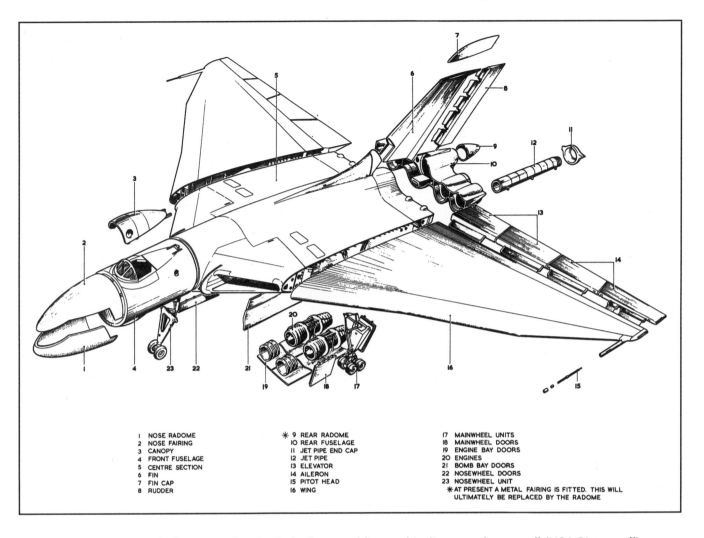

I	NOSE RADOME	✳ 9	REAR RADOME	17	MAINWHEEL UNITS
2	NOSE FAIRING	10	REAR FUSELAGE	18	MAINWHEEL DOORS
3	CANOPY	11	JET PIPE END CAP	19	ENGINE BAY DOORS
4	FRONT FUSELAGE	12	JET PIPE	20	ENGINES
5	CENTRE SECTION	13	ELEVATOR	21	BOMB BAY DOORS
6	FIN	14	AILERON	22	NOSEWHEEL DOORS
7	FIN CAP	15	PITOT HEAD	23	NOSEWHEEL UNIT
8	RUDDER	16	WING	✳	AT PRESENT A METAL FAIRING IS FITTED. THIS WILL ULTIMATELY BE REPLACED BY THE RADOME

The Vulcan B.1 consisted of a series of major jig built assemblies as this diagram shows well. (HSA Bitteswell)

workable ideas included the provision of ejection seats for all crew members or for the whole front fuselage to be ejected as a capsule. Both were eventually axed due to the development and engineering costs involved.

Although the tragic loss of the crew of XA897 stunned all involved with the Vulcan programme, the subsequent vindication of the aircraft meant that deliveries could resume to 230 OCU. Crews destined for the Vulcan came from a predominantly bomber background.

The pilots were mainly from the Canberra fleet whilst the navigators were drawn from Canberra, Washington or Lincoln units. The theory behind drawing the navigators from these particular aircraft lies in the fact that all were familiar with much of the equipment built into the Vulcan, albeit most was of a later marque. Primary bombing and navigation was handled by the H2S radar system which was very much a two-pronged instrument capable of carrying out both tasks with equal aplomb. When in pure bombing mode it was frequently referred to as the BNS, whilst in bombing and navigation mode it was called NBS. The basic components in the system were the H2S Mk.9A radar plus the Nav Bomb System Mk.1 and the Nav Bomb Comp.Mk2. Integrated with the basic radar system was the APQ13 navigational aid which came complete with a "handle like eggs" sticker. Most of the avionics was developed from equipment already in service although the introduction of Green Satin, a Decca Doppler unit, ensured that both navigators had a high workload at times. As the name suggests, Green Satin used the Doppler principle to calculate the aircraft's true ground speed and drift. This information was then fed into an analogue computer which then generated a display of the aircraft's position as geographical coordinates. One other important piece of navigational equipment was also carried in the Vulcan – namely a periscope sextant. Used

for astro-navigation in the event of main equipment failure, a mounting for the sextant was available on either side of the cabin. The newest category of aircrew member in the Vulcan crew was the AEO, all the others coming from established branches.

Originally it was intended that NCO signalers would transfer across to the new bomber, however this concept was soon modified when the subject of ECM was brought into the equation. Although at an embryonic stage in development it was realised that a greater depth of knowledge would be required for the new crew member, much of it beyond the education of many of the old style signals branch. Some NCOs showed the aptitude to convert to the new position and were later integrated into the early crews. Although the Vulcans of Bomber Command had no ECM fitted, this did not stop the intensive training of the fledgling AEO's in its use when it was finally installed. Until the advent of the B.1A and its ECM tailcone the AEO relied upon the chaff dispensers fitted behind the main gear bays for protection. For use in the tail warning radar slot a system known as "Red Garter" was employed on a few aircraft. Based upon the Orange Putter system earlier fitted to the Canberra it used an 18 inch scanner which under ideal conditions gave indications of aircraft approaching within 170 degrees azimuth and 80

The Vulcan B.1 undercarriage was an impressive feat of engineering with much of the works hidden within the leg. The cycle of retraction is also illustrated in this diagram and reveals that the bogie sits on top of the leg when retracted. (BAe/Avro Heritage)

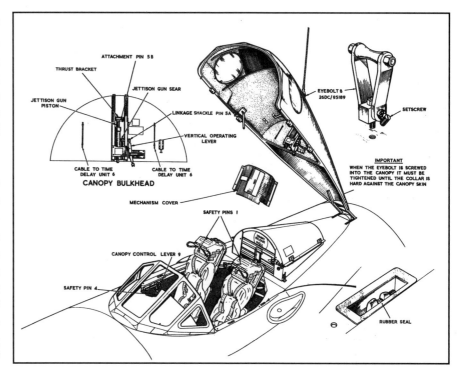

For access during ground maintenance, the Vulcan's canopy required a crane to assist in removal. However in an emergency the canopy could either be ejected by selection of the release handles on the canopy rails or by either pilot beginning the ejection seat sequence. There was also a ground emergency handle on the port nose. Departure was aided by a canopy gun located on the rear bulkhead behind the pilots. (HSA Bitteswell)

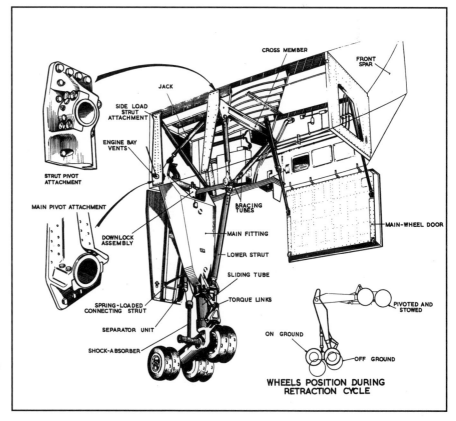

degrees elevation. In actual service the TWR found little favour due to shortcomings in its performance and was therefore rarely used. Thus the Vulcan had to rely upon its height, speed, and bundles of chaff/window until aircraft capable ECM systems were available. Whilst every effort was being made by industry and the TRE and RAE to engineer satisfactory equipment for the Vulcan and the other "V" bombers, the conversion of crews and the creation of operating squadrons continued.

The first squadron to form was No. 83 Sqdn on 20 May 1957. After the initial workup period, two aircraft were dispatched to the United States to take part in the SAC Bombing, Navigation, and Reconnaissance competition held at Pinecastle AFB. Throughout the month of October the squadrons crews applied themselves diligently to the various exercises within the competition known

as "Iron Horse" to USAF and "Operation Longshot" to the RAF. Later as the bomber fleets of both countries reached their zenith, it became better known as "Giant Voice" when held in the USA and "Double Top" in its UK format.

The introduction of a completely new aircraft type to squadron service invariably brings its crop of accidents. Such a fate befell XA908 of 83 Sqdn on 24 October 1958. Undertaking a Lone Ranger exercise routed via Goose Bay in Labrador, the Vulcan was en route to Lincoln AFB, Nebraska. At 35,000 ft. above Dresden, 60 miles north of Detroit, the aircraft suffered total electrical failure. System backup was provided by an emergency battery which in theory could provide enough power to drive the essential electrical services for at least twenty minutes. For reasons that later became clear, the power was totally drained after three min-

utes which resulted in the PFCU solenoid valves locking the flight controls irreversibly. The resulting crash killed all six on board although the co-pilot had ejected clear – he drowned after landing in Lake St.Clair minus a lifejacket. Accident investigators finally established the cause when a similar incident befell a Vulcan a few days later. Fortunately this time the aircraft was sitting on the ground. Main power supplies to run the airframe and particularly the essential services such as the PFCUs were provided by four engine driven 112v DC generators. These in turn were linked to one main busbar. A short circuit across this single item had totally isolated the aircraft from its power supplies thus causing the crash. After this tragedy the busbar on all the B.1 aircraft and the subsequent B.2 variant was divided and assembled as two individual sections.

Another area of the aircraft and its operations that had given cause for concern was the damage created by engine failure. Due to the parallel nature of the Vulcan's paired engines, there is a marked tendency for the failed ECU to eject its compressor blades forward from the intake where they are caught by the airflow being drawn into the engine next door – the consequence of this is extensive damage to both powerplants. Although not a common occurrence, the severity of the damage plus the risk to both crew and aircraft prompted Avro to put forward a series of modifications that were planned to suppress the sideways movement of exploding engine parts. It was intended that the modifications would help contain some of the excess damage caused to the airframe and its fuel system as it was

Vulcan B.1 XA911 reveals that at the tip of its rear fuselage is the radome for the "Red Gator" tail warning radar. Due to technical problems it is highly unlikely that the system was ever installed. Under the starboard wing is a hangar fire dolly more commonly known as a "Dalek." This was connected into the aircraft's fire suppression system and could initiate the extinguishers from outside in the event of a fire. (C. P. Russell-Smith Collection)

This next sequence of photos reveals the extent of the strength of the Vulcan airframe. On 20 October 1959, XH498 of 617 Sqdn severely damaged its main left gear after attempting a touch down at Wellington airport in New Zealand. Unable to evacuate the rear crew due to the extended gear the captain flew the aircraft onto Okahea. (C. P. Russell-Smith Collection)

After the gentlest of touch downs XH498 came to rest with its TBC still deployed. To escape from the aircraft after an emergency shutdown the crew ejected the canopy and managed safe egress via the dropped wing. (Bob Mitchell Collection)

Apart from the damage caused to the port wing the Vulcan was in remarkably good condition. The play of the light under the wings reveals the complex curves introduced into the leading edges when the wing was redesigned to encompass Phase 2. XH498 was repaired in New Zealand, later flying home to the UK. (Bob Mitchell Collection)

When parked up for a long time it was advisable to place the intake and exhaust blanks into position to reduce the possibility of FOD entering the intakes especially. Vulcan B.1A XH475, still wearing the finish associated with the high level strike role, is on a visit to Aldergrove. (C. P. Russell-Smith Collection)

The Vulcan engines' need for mass air flow is apparent in this shot of XH480 which reveals the size of the aircraft's intakes and the ground equipment needed to reach them. (C. P. Russell-Smith Collection)

The operating jacks for the conventional bomb doors are located on the front and rear bulkheads and are hydraulically driven. The intermediate jacks are unconnected to the aircraft's system being used for steadying purposes only. (HSA Bitteswell)

recognised that there was no adequate defence against the disintegrating compressor problem.

Accidents notwithstanding, the Vulcan B1 continued to re-equip the various Bomber Command units slated to receive it. No. 101 Sqdn reformed as a Vulcan operator at RAF Finningly on 15 October 1957

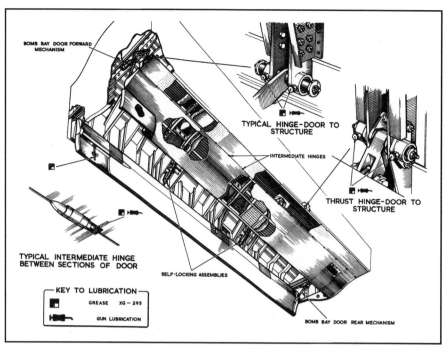

The Vulcan centre section was composed of subassemblies which when joined together produced a very strong structure more than capable of carrying any load. This diagram illustrates the assemblage of the B.1 airframe. (BAe/Avro Heritage)

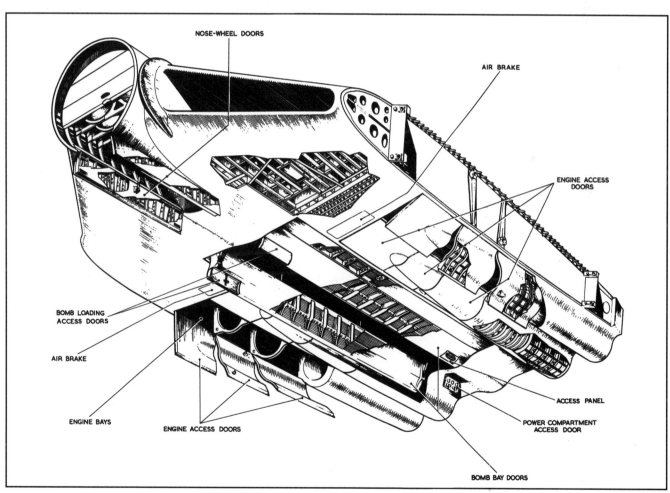

By 1964, Vulcan XH503 had been fully upgraded to B.1A status, the extra length of the nose gear compared to the later B.2 is worthy of note. It was intended that this slightly nose up stance would assist the Vulcan during take-off by presenting the leading edge at a more favourable angle to the airflow. (C. P. Russell-Smith Collection)

having previously operated the Canberra. It was quickly followed by that most famous RAF bomber squadron, No. 617 "The Dambusters" who accepted their first Vulcans in May 1958 after trading in their Canberras.

The foregoing trials and tribulations notwithstanding, the Vulcans of Bomber Command settled into a routine which involved close cooperation with their counterparts in SAC. Training exercises involving dummy nuclear weapons or "shapes" were the order of the day. Vulcans trained not only with the standard British weapon, the MC Mk.1 *Blue Danube*, but with the American equivalent of which the aircraft could carry two.

However this was an era where behind the scenes political upheaval finally culminated in the infamous 1957 Defence White Paper presented to the House Of Commons by the Defence Minster of the day, Duncan Sandys. The basic credo contained within this paper proposed to eliminate the manned aircraft entirely from the British defence scene and replace the whole lot with a variety of missiles optimised for defence or offensive purposes. Fortunately common-sense prevailed and this ludicrous piece of tomfoolery was eventually consigned to the dustbin of history. The effect on the British aircraft industry was not so easily overcome as overseas tours to show off the latest in aviation technology were either cancelled by the recipient countries or the companies themselves, both English Electric and Avro were affected in this way.

Fortunately the delays to the Vulcan programme were negated to minimal and the development of the basic design towards the far more capable B.2 continued. The new version of the Vulcan began to enter squadron service in 1960 when 34 of the earlier B.1 were still in RAF use. As these aircraft were only a few years old it was decided to incorporate some of the B.2 features into these airframes in order to extend their useful working lives. To this end the most visible modifi-

PARACHUTE STOWAGE COMPARTMENT

PARACHUTE JETTISON HOOK

TAIL CONE

JET PIPE TUNNELS

JET PIPE END CAPS (DETACHABLE)

INBOARD ENGINE RIB

TUNNEL OMITTED TO SHOW STRUCTURE

CENTRE ENGINE RIB

JET PIPE GUIDE RAIL

OUTBOARD ENGINE RIB

The original Vulcan tailcone was a short pointed affair with the brake parachute mounted in a compartment on the side. A later modification applied to a few aircraft introduced the Red Gator radar behind a fibreglass tailcone in place of the original metal one. (BAe/Avro Heritage)

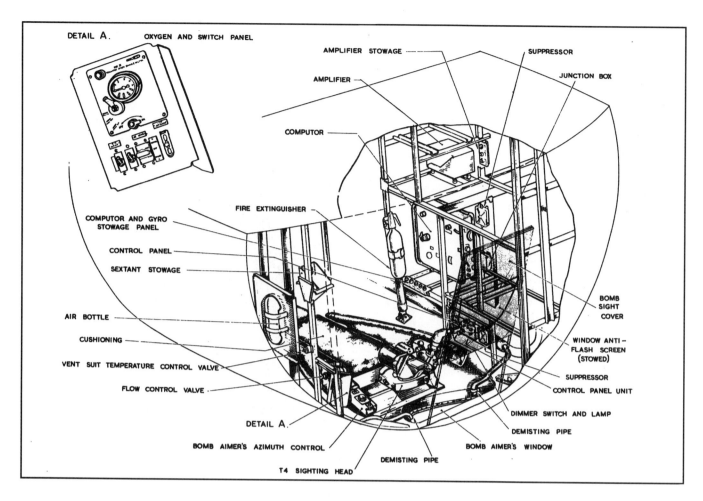

DETAIL A. OXYGEN AND SWITCH PANEL

AMPLIFIER STOWAGE SUPPRESSOR

AMPLIFIER JUNCTION BOX

COMPUTOR

FIRE EXTINGUISHER

COMPUTOR AND GYRO STOWAGE PANEL

CONTROL PANEL

SEXTANT STOWAGE

AIR BOTTLE

CUSHIONING

VENT SUIT TEMPERATURE CONTROL VALVE

FLOW CONTROL VALVE

DETAIL A.

BOMB AIMER'S AZIMUTH CONTROL

T4 SIGHTING HEAD

DEMISTING PIPE

BOMB AIMER'S WINDOW

DEMISTING PIPE

DIMMER SWITCH AND LAMP

CONTROL PANEL UNIT

SUPPRESSOR

WINDOW ANTI-FLASH SCREEN (STOWED)

BOMB SIGHT COVER

The bomb aimer's position originally housed a T4 bombsight when the aircraft was first built. As the H2S became more reliable the need for visual bombing was no longer needed, therefore the sight was removed and its pneumatic system was linked into that of the entrance door. In place of the bomb sight came an F.95 strike recording camera. (NATO AM)

cation was applied to the rear fuselage. This bulged extension increased the aircraft's overall length by 2 ft. 10 ins. and required the relocation of the tail warning skid and tail brake chute. A foreshortening of the rudder was also required. Contained within the rear fuselage bulge were the ECM cans, transmitters, and power units in equal proportion, and the water glycol/VCCP cooling system. At the very tip was housed the definitive tail warning radar, the Red Steer Mk.1. From the surviving fleet 29 aircraft were progressively withdrawn for rework. As the power supplies for the ECM units were rated at 200v AC and the B.1 used 112v DC

as its main power supply, an extra engine driven alternator was installed to cover this demand. The prime contractor for the conversion programme was Armstrong Whitworth which like Avro was by now a constituent member of the Hawker Siddeley Group. The final redelivery of a redesignated B.1A was accomplished on 6 March 1963 bringing an end to a programme that had taken 32 months to complete.

In order to cope with the logistics required to cater for two different variants of the same aircraft, it was decided that the Vulcan B.1As and the few remaining B.1s of Nos. 44, 50, and 101 Squadrons would all be

allocated to the same base in Lincolnshire, RAF Waddington.

One further major modification carried out on the B.1s was the fitment of an in-flight refuelling probe to extend the available range. For this purpose the fleet arrived at the home airfield of Flight Refuelling Ltd. at Tarrent Rushton during 1963 where the required probe, lighting, and pipework was installed.

It was during this period that changes were made to the role of the Vulcan B.1 squadrons. Initially charged with nuclear (strike) weapons delivery, their role gradually became one of conventional

When ECM was finally fitted to the Vulcan, it was housed in a bulged rear fuselage. Given that the equipment was mainly valve powered a reasonable heat exchanging system was required. This consisted of water glycol which was pumped round the cooling pipelines before passing through the VCCP which vented the heat off into the atmosphere via the matrix mounted under the shroud on the rear fuselage. (Ray Deacon)

attack using standard 1,000 lbs. iron bombs, the nuclear role passing to their newer siblings. This state of affairs was not to last long however as in 1966 the B.1 began to leave RAF service as Bomber Command began to concentrate all its effort on the vastly more capable Vulcan B.2. By the end of 1967, the Vulcan B.1 was no longer included in the inventory of the RAF except in the role of training aids.

During its service life and for some time after, this first Vulcan variant also played a vital role in aircraft development, not only for the Vulcan, but for the British aircraft industry in general.

Areas that the test aircraft were primarily involved in included engines, weapons, avionics, and other equipment. In 1958, B.1 XA902 was allocated to Rolls Royce with whom it was first employed on flying trials concerning the Conway11 powerplant. After two years the aircraft was grounded and the Conways were replaced by the later Spey. It continued in this vital support role until finally withdrawn from use in 1962. Another Vulcan was also allocated to powerplant development, this being XA894 which arrived at Bristol Patchway where the Olympus 22R engine and an associated fuel tank were mounted into and under the bomb bay, the engine being contained within a mock up nacelle. The purpose of these flight trials was to clear the engine for the forthcoming, but ill-fated TSR2 multi-role aircraft. These tests were to come to an abrupt end on 3 December 1962. During a full reheat run of the Olympus 22R on the ground, the engine suffered a major failure which caused serious damage to the attendant fuel system. The subsequent conflagration totally destroyed the aircraft although there were no casualties. Following the ill-starred XA894 was another B.1, XA903 which had recently completed an extensive selection of Blue Steel missile trials for Avro. This Vulcan joined the Patchway fleet in January 1964 where, after a major overhaul, an Olympus 593 engine, destined to power Concorde, was fitted in an aerodynamic nacelle under the fuselage. Such was the modification state of this test bed aircraft that RAF Vulcan crews would have had difficulty in recognising it internally. Extra tanks for fuel were fitted into the bomb bay as were water tanks. These were connected to an icing rig whose frame was located under the nose

where its addition had meant that the defunct bomb aimers blister had been removed. Further equipment was fitted into the cockpit so that monitoring of the test engine in all aspects of flight could be recorded.

First flight of XA903 in its new role took place on 9 September 1966 and the converted bomber was retained for Olympus trials until 21 July 1971. By this time all of the variants of the Concorde engine had been tested in the air which represented 219 test flights and 248 running hours.

From Bristol, XA903 was trans-

Still awaiting conversion to B.1A status, XA913 has already visited Flight Refuelling Ltd. at Tarrent Rushton to have the flight refuelling system installed. (C. P. Russell-Smith Collection)

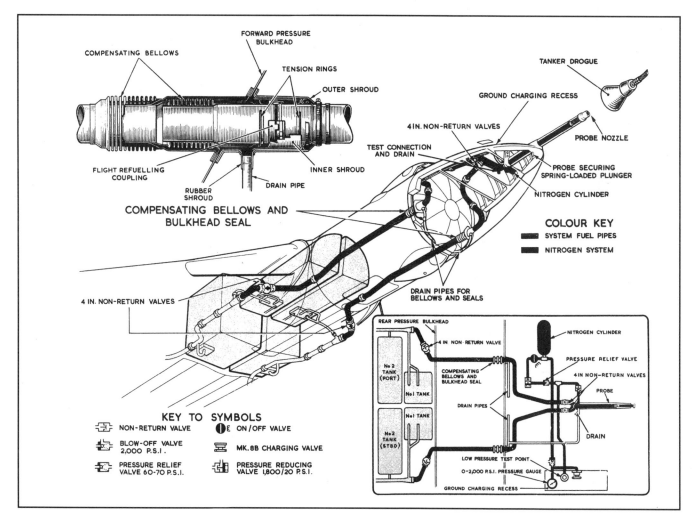

The introduction of the flight refuelling system did extend its range although problems were experienced with leaks at the bulkhead bellows. (BAe/Avro Heritage)

ferred to Marshalls of Cambridge where it was modified for the RB199 engine programme. Destined to power the multi-nation Tornado this powerplant was installed in an aerodynamic half fuselage under the bomb bay. Such was the extent of the detail in this part fuselage that a Mauser 27mm cannon plus 150 rounds was installed to test the effects of gas ingestion on the engine and its performance. From 19 April 1973 until its final flight was made on 18 August 1978, the Vulcan undertook 125 flights over a period of 203 hours. Final official withdrawal date of this most modified of Vulcans was 27 February 1977 when it was flown to RAE Farnborough for disposal.

Having just rotated after a roller landing this undershot of XA896 reveals the gear cycling to the closed position and the electrically driven airbrakes retracting. This particular aircraft was later partially converted to test the BS 100 vectored thrust engine before the project was summarily cancelled. (C. P. Russell-Smith Collection)

Remarkably still in an all over silver finish, XA895 reveals that it has undergone all the modification required to bring it up to B.1A standard. The flight refuelling system was added by Flight Refuelling at a later date under a separate contract. (Ray Deacon)

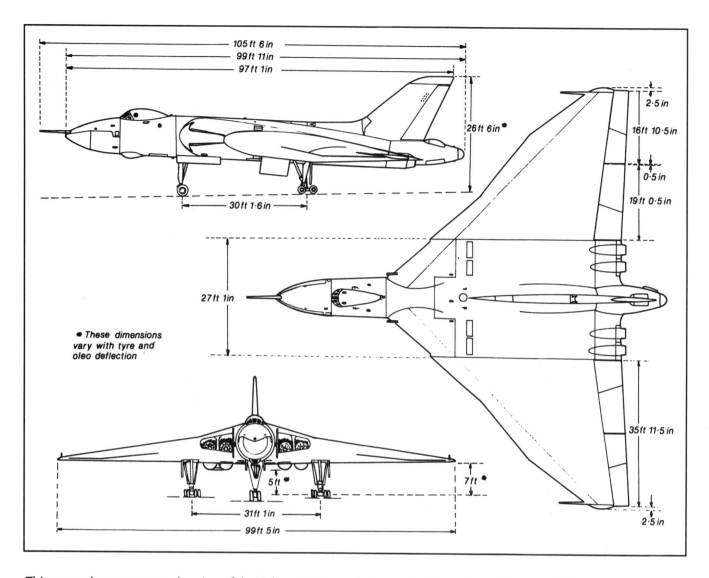

105 ft 6 in
99 ft 11 in
97 ft 1 in

26 ft 6 in *

30 ft 1·6 in

2·5 in
16 ft 10·5 in
0·5 in
19 ft 0·5 in

27 ft 1 in

* These dimensions
vary with tyre and
oleo deflection

35 ft 11·5 in

5 ft *
7 ft *

31 ft 1 in

99 ft 5 in

2·5 in

This general arrangement drawing of the Vulcan B.1A reveals the major dimensions of the aircraft. (BAe/Avro Heritage)

The height of the Vulcans stance shows well as B.1 XH482 is towed behind a Rolls Royce powered tug unit. The interconnecting towbar was reckoned to be a one-man unit which needed at least three people to fit! (C. P. Russell-Smith Collection)

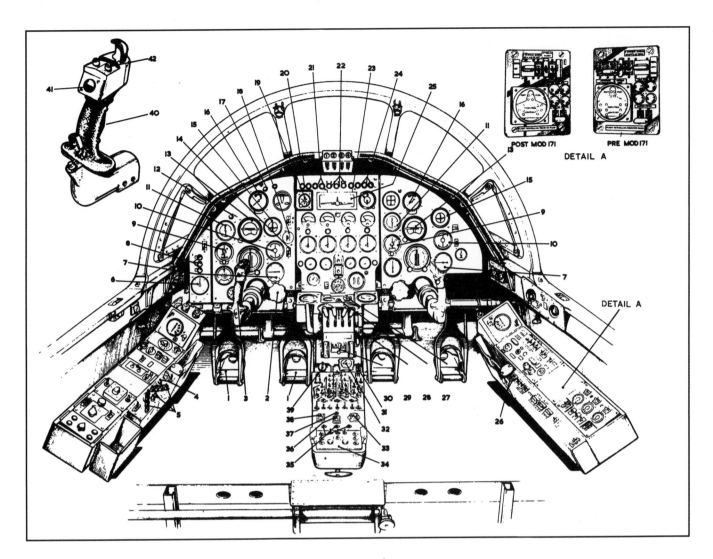

The Vulcan cockpit evolved over a period of time from the original in the Type 698 to this version in the B.1. Modification 171 introduced a modified refuel panel at the co-pilot's position with the flight refuelling lights added. (BAe/Avro Heritage)

As expected for an aircraft that stood so high from the ground, many of the access panels were located underneath the aircraft. Those located on the upper surface included the brilliantly named "break in drag off panels" used for connecting chains to a Vulcan after a belly landing. (BAe/Avro Heritage)

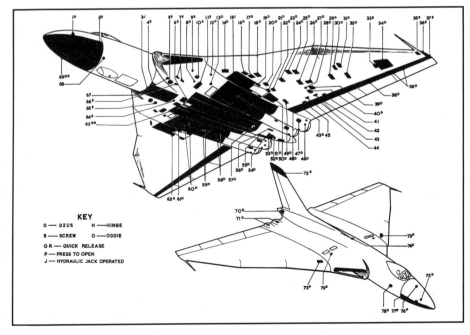

KEY

D — DZUS   H — HINGE
S — SCREW   O — ODDIE
Q R — QUICK RELEASE
P — PRESS TO OPEN
J — HYDRAULIC JACK OPERATED

EXTENDING 4 THE OPTIONS

At first glance to the casual observer there are marked family similarities between the Vulcan B.1A and its successor the B.2. However such observations are purely cosmetic in nature as under the skin a very different aircraft lurked.

The origins of the Vulcan B.2 can be traced back to 1954 when the Air Staff issued the very optimistic OR 330 intended as a proposal for the development of a long range reconnaissance aircraft with a secondary bombing role. The proposal outlines required this venture to be capable of Mach 2.5 at an altitude of 60,000 ft. with a basic range of 5,000 miles. A further refinement, coupled with increased definition of the aircraft required, finally resulted in the appearance of Spec R156T. The challenge to build such a machine was taken up by Vickers, Handley-Page, and of course Avro. The latter's project was referred to as the Type 730 and was continually under development until 1957 when the Defence White Paper for that year appeared. This being a product of its time it proposed to replace all manned military aircraft with a raft of missile types to defend the UK. Ongoing cutting edge projects such as the Type 730

Vulcan centre fuselages move along the line at Chadderton. In the bay next door the intake sections that form another part in the process keep pace. The openings clearly showing in the nearest fuselage are the upper fuel system vents. The second fuselage section already has its airbrakes installed and these are deployed in the mid position. Pilots frequently commented that they were only effective when fully extended.(BAe/Avro Heritage)

Close to completion on the assembly line this view of in production Vulcans reveals a wealth of detail. Observe the split in the flying control surfaces and the capaciousness of the brake chute bay. (BAe/Avro Heritage)

fell victims to its proponents axe and this programme along with so many others literally disappeared overnight. One of the consequences of such thinking was the insistence that extant parts of these projects be destroyed immediately, thus the already fabricated parts of

the Type 730 ended their lives at Woodford as scrap metal bins.

With its hopes of a supersonic reconnaissance/bomber finally dashed, the RAF began to take a fresh and closer look at the aircraft already in the inventory. From the

point of view of the Chief Designer at Avro, Roy Evans, there was plenty of development growth left in the Vulcan design, this having been built in during the planning and definition stages of the aircraft's gestation. During the consultation process the Avro team realised that

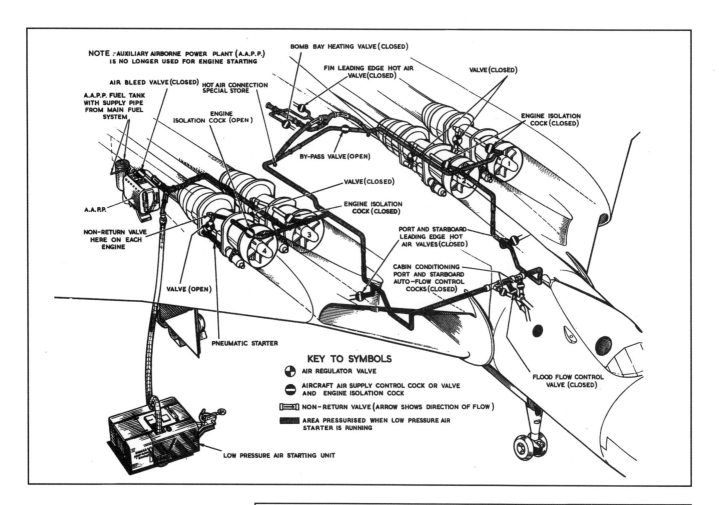

NOTE :-AUXILIARY AIRBORNE POWER PLANT (A.A.P.P.) IS NO LONGER USED FOR ENGINE STARTING

BOMB BAY HEATING VALVE (CLOSED)

FIN LEADING EDGE HOT AIR VALVE (CLOSED)

VALVE (CLOSED)

AIR BLEED VALVE (CLOSED)

HOT AIR CONNECTION SPECIAL STORE

A.A.P.P. FUEL TANK WITH SUPPLY PIPE FROM MAIN FUEL SYSTEM

ENGINE ISOLATION COCK (OPEN)

ENGINE ISOLATION COCK (CLOSED)

BY-PASS VALVE (OPEN)

A.A.P.P.

VALVE (CLOSED)

ENGINE ISOLATION COCK (CLOSED)

NON-RETURN VALVE HERE ON EACH ENGINE

PORT AND STARBOARD LEADING EDGE HOT AIR VALVES (CLOSED)

CABIN CONDITIONING PORT AND STARBOARD AUTO-FLOW CONTROL COCKS (CLOSED)

VALVE (OPEN)

PNEUMATIC STARTER

FLOOD FLOW CONTROL VALVE (CLOSED)

KEY TO SYMBOLS

⊕ AIR REGULATOR VALVE

⊖ AIRCRAFT AIR SUPPLY CONTROL COCK OR VALVE AND ENGINE ISOLATION COCK

▣ NON-RETURN VALVE (ARROW SHOWS DIRECTION OF FLOW)

▬ AREA PRESSURISED WHEN LOW PRESSURE AIR STARTER IS RUNNING

LOW PRESSURE AIR STARTING UNIT

The Vulcan featured a very versatile engine starting system. Only one needed starting before the throttle was opened to 80%. If the reason was a scramble all the cross feed valves were opened and the remaining three ECUs could be spun up at the same time. Starting could also be carried out using a Palouste air starting unit or the rapid air starting system. (NATO AM)

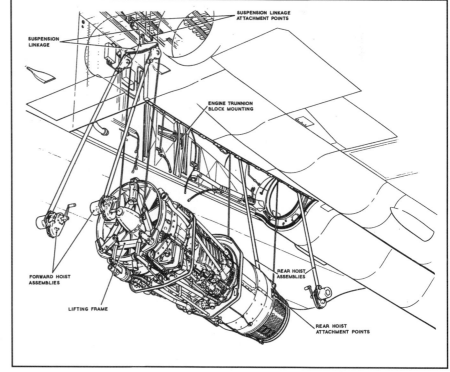

SUSPENSION LINKAGE ATTACHMENT POINTS

SUSPENSION LINKAGE

ENGINE TRUNNION BLOCK MOUNTING

FORWARD HOIST ASSEMBLIES

LIFTING FRAME

REAR HOIST ASSEMBLIES

REAR HOIST ATTACHMENT POINTS

The Olympus engines in the Vulcan were held in by two pins through the trunnion blocks and a bolt on top of the compressor casing. This method shows four winches being used to remove the engine although there was provision for the use of three winches only. To remove an engine all the services needed disconnecting – the jet pipe was slid back and the intake make up pieces were removed. (NATO AM)

Seen from underneath, this shot reveals the size of the bomb bay which in this case is empty. The bulges on the outboard wings are the covers for the PFCUs and the segmentation of the flight control surfaces is clearly visible. (C. P. Russell-Smith Collection)

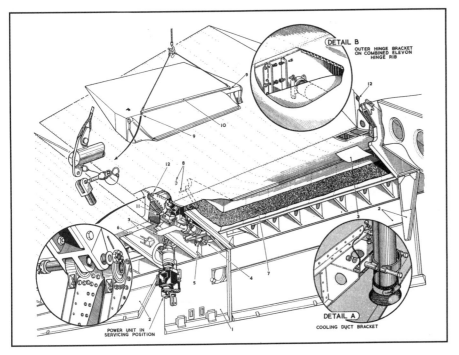

Under normal circumstances the PFCUs that drive the inner sections of the elevons are hidden beneath the external access panels. Being independent of the main hydraulic system they occasionally required attention for their reservoirs to be replenished. (NATO AM)

Bomber Command would require even more flexibility from an improved Vulcan. Thus one of their first moves was to increase the wing span from 99 ft. to 111 ft., the maximum size that the standard airfield hangars could take. An extension in span brought about an increase in wing area from 3,446 sq.ft. to 3,965 sq.ft. all without increasing the wing loading. This gave a lift coefficient of 0.45 at an improved buffet threshold cruise Mach of 0.873. The proposed changes to the wing were submitted to the MoS in draft form in September 1955 and were followed in return by a production order for 17 aircraft which was dated for 30 September 1954. Astute readers will note that this contract is the same number as the last one for the B.1. This is due to the fact that the remaining aircraft of the B.1 order were changed to B.2 whilst on the production line and the first had progressed enough to feature the original smaller intakes of the earlier model. The definitive Vulcan centre sections of the B.2 featured larger intakes capable of handling the increased mass air flow that would be required for the Olympus 301 engine. This revamped B.1 contract was quickly followed by a further one for eight aircraft whilst a third called for 24 Vulcan B.2s on 25 February 1956. A final batch of 40 aircraft were ordered on 22 January 1958. Allied to the revamped wing, by now christened the Phase 2C, came a proposal to install more powerful RR(BS) Olympus 200 series engines rated at 16,000 lbs. st. each. Originally known as the Olympus B.O.16 the new engine featured a redesigned compressor which had fewer stages but had increased mass air flow. The thrust starting point for this engine was promised at 15,000 lbs. st. plus

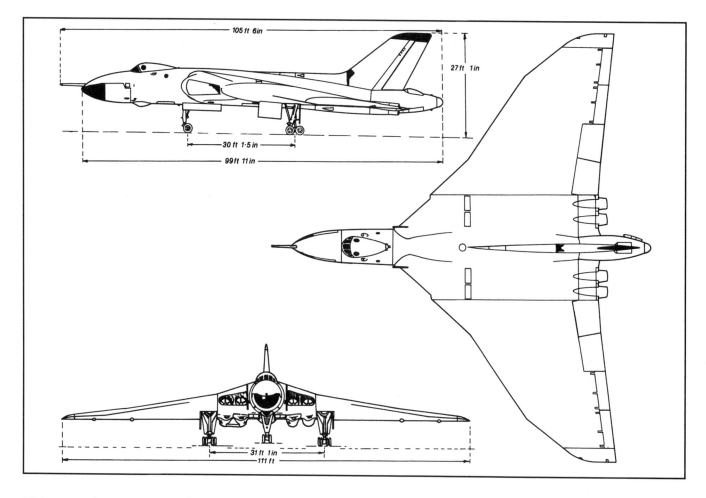

105 ft 6in
27 ft 1 in
30 ft 1·5 in
99 ft 11 in
31 ft 1 in
111 ft

This general arrangement diagram of the Vulcan B.2 shows well the development that took place to create the Phase 2C wing. Of note on the diagram is the slightly lowered nose stance associated with this variant. (HSA Bitteswell)

whilst the projected B.0.121 was initially rated, on paper at least, at 20,000 lbs. st.

Taking all these changes into account, it was confidently forecast that the improved Vulcan B.2 would have increased range and better height capabilities, far better than that of the in service B.1 which at full load was stuck at a maximum altitude of 43,000 ft.

Testing of the new wing plan form was entrusted to the surviving second prototype upon which conversion work began in August 1956. Other major changes included full span elevons along the trailing edge in place of the separate

ailerons and elevators previously fitted. All the PFCUs became independent units whose only connection to the airframe was electro mechanical as the required hydraulic fluid was contained in individual reservoirs. Because of the changes to the control system and its method of operation, artificial feel units were installed to cover all three axes of flight-control, surface positioning after input being the responsibility of a mixer box. First flight of VX777 took place on 31 August 1957 which was followed by an appearance at that years SBAC show. Test flying revealed that the new wing improved the aircraft's range by about 25-30% and its height capabilities were

summed up by an entry in the Vulcan B.2 Aircrew Manual which read, "There is no height restriction on the aircraft because of airframe limitations." Further aerodynamic trials and general handling occupied the aircraft until 1960 when it was transferred to RAE Farnborough for runway brake tests. Three years later the usefulness of VX777 was deemed over and it was scrapped.

Powerplant development and test flying of the Olympus series 200 ECUs was the province of Vulcan B.1 XA891 which began its work in early 1958. However the aircraft's test career was cut short when it was lost in a crash at Walkington near Hull on 24 July 1959 when the electrical systems failed. This is another area in which the Mk.2 airframe underwent a radical shake-up. Very much an electrical aircraft, the Vulcan enclosed some 102 electric motors and actuators within its airframe. Thus the change to to the less bulky 200v AC system from the earlier 112v DC system was to be welcomed. Power generation was by an alternator mounted on each engine which received its drive via a CSDU. Secondary power supplies were courtesy of 28v DC whilst the few remaining items of equipment that could not be converted from 112v DC received their required power supplies via a bank of TRUs located on the cabin floor. To trial the proposed electrical system and clear it for RAF service, a Vulcan B.1

XA893 had a partial system installed in one wing. No obvious problems were encountered during these trials and the programme was adjudged a complete success. One other modification applied to the B.2 was the deletion of the hydraulic pump from No.4 ECU. The other engines retained a pump each to a new and improved design thus a fourth would have been excessive.

All of these modifications were finally embodied in one airframe – the first production Vulcan B.2 XH533 which had been undergoing construction on the Woodford production line as part of an earlier B.1 contract. First flown on 19 August 1958, the new bomber featured the

new wing, toed out jet pipes, strengthened main gear legs, and a shortened nose leg. Allied to the revamped electrical system was the installation of an AAPP which provided the aircraft with a measure of independence as it could power all the required electrics and initialise engine start. This latter feature was later deleted as it was found to be overstraining the AAPP and had been superseded by the rapid air start system. To further maintain emergency power to the controls and other vital systems, a Plessey built ram air turbine was located under the port intake. It was intended that this should be lowered should the aircraft lose all electrical power including that from the on board 28v DC battery.

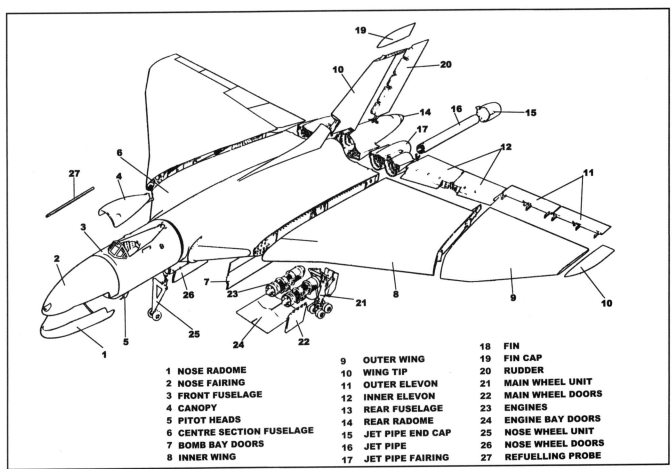

1	NOSE RADOME	18	FIN
2	NOSE FAIRING	19	FIN CAP
3	FRONT FUSELAGE	20	RUDDER
4	CANOPY	21	MAIN WHEEL UNIT
5	PITOT HEADS	22	MAIN WHEEL DOORS
6	CENTRE SECTION FUSELAGE	23	ENGINES
7	BOMB BAY DOORS	24	ENGINE BAY DOORS
8	INNER WING	25	NOSE WHEEL UNIT
9	OUTER WING	26	NOSE WHEEL DOORS
10	WING TIP	27	REFUELLING PROBE
11	OUTER ELEVON		
12	INNER ELEVON		
13	REAR FUSELAGE		
14	REAR RADOME		
15	JET PIPE END CAP		
16	JET PIPE		
17	JET PIPE FAIRING		

Comparison between this diagram and the earlier one for the B.1 shows that the B.2 was very much an evolutionary step not a radical redesign. (HSA Bitteswell)

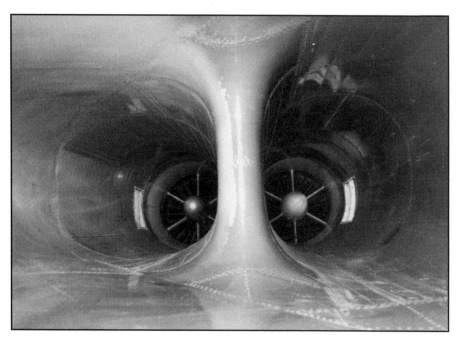

Due to the mass air flow requirements of the Olympus engines the resulting intakes were easy to enter for inspection purposes. The powerplants facing us here are Mk301 ECUs – those of the earlier Mk201 variety were slightly smaller in diameter and had a longer nose bullet. They also required more tapered intake make up pieces to blend them into the intakes. (Damien Burke)

To further improve the Vulcan's effectiveness an emergency hydraulic power pack was added. Located in the bomb bay roof, the EHPP had its own reservoir and was capable of opening the bomb doors as long as selector power was available. Thus we have the scenario of a Vulcan with electrical power being supplied by a RAT and its vital hydraulics, the bomb doors, being operated by the EHPP. At a later stage in the aircraft's career, a switch was placed in the power compartment that could transfer the ECM system onto the vital supplies busbar thus giving the aircraft some protection during its attack run. As first flown XH533 lacked the bulged tailcone that was required to house the ECM transmitters and power units plus the Red Steer TWR. This was a later addition to this airframe which occurred during the B.1 conversion programme. Although missing its defensive avionics, the remainder of the aircraft was put through an intensive trials programme which revealed the improvement in handling and performance granted by the new wing. To demonstrate the effective- ness of the design a new operational altitude of 61,500 ft. was achieved during these trials.

Defensive electronics was an area that desperately needed to be addressed given the improvements that were taking place in the Soviet air defence and detection network. Originally the defence system had been easily jammed by the use of window/chaff, however the deploy- ment of multi-band radar had ren-

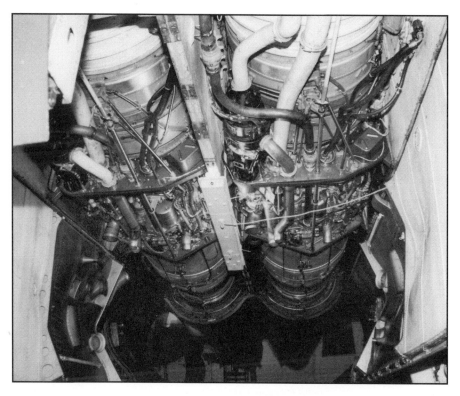

The opened engine doors for Nos. 1 and 2 ECUs reveals much of the detail on the Olympus engine and its services. On the left are the alternators and their cooling pipes – directly behind on the dividing bulkhead is the CSDU which drove the ancillaries. On the right hand side is the engine oil tank whilst just in front are the connections to the airframes hydraulic system. (Damien Burke)

The throttle box for the Olympus engines dominates this view of the pilot's panel. Just in shot is the drop down console housing the fuel system controls. The sparcity of vision afforded the pilots is also clearly seen in this view. The small triangular window at the bottom of the windscreen is the direct vision window which could cause problems with pressurisation if not properly secured. Dominating the coaming are the RAT handle and just below it the four warning extinguishant buttons for the engines. (Damien Burke)

The panel that normally sits under the airbrakes has been removed to reveal the cooling pipes underneath – in front of the airbrake is the ram air cooling intake. (Damien Burke)

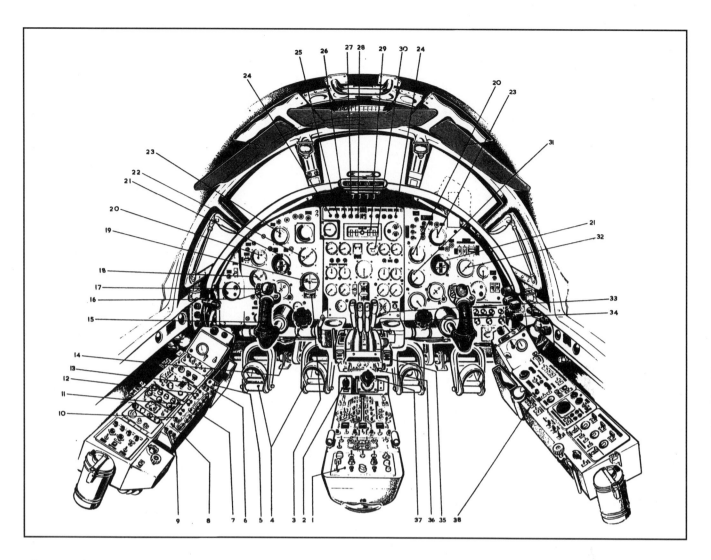

The panels presented to the pilots covered a multitude of tasks. The console on the left enabled the captain to control engine start, PFCU start, and bomb door opening amongst other functions. The opposite console for the co-pilot controlled flight refuelling and cabin pressurisation and air conditioning. Directly in front of both pilots the centre panel presented instruments to both whilst each had a set of primary instruments. (HSA Bitteswell)

dered that system of limited use-fullness. Also desperately needed was a tail warning radar, the previously trailed Red Garter on the B.1 having proven ineffective. To remedy these deficiencies, various government departments were engaged in developing the required equipment. When the modified rear fuselage was finally incorporated from new in the B.2, it contained an ARI 5919(later ARI 5929) Red Steer TWR which had been developed from the AI.13 interceptor set that which had originally graced the nose of the

Gloster Meteor NF.11 and NF.14 night fighters.

The new ECM systems were entirely noise generator based and were capable of dealing with the Soviet fighter control systems extant in the 1950s which used a total of four waveband ranges for detection, command, control, and interception guidance. The kit itself appears as large black cans – two per jamming system. One housed the power supply unit whilst the other housed the mainly valve-based jammer. To cool the cans which

generated enormous amounts of heat a pump powered water glycol system was used. This in turn was passed through a vapour cycle cooling pack which vented the excess heat to atmosphere via a heat exchanger also mounted in the rear fuselage. The creation of the new rear fuselage also resulted in the relocation of the TBC. Initially on the Vulcan B.1 it had been located behind a door on the starboard side of the short rear fuselage. The new empennage required that the TBC be placed in a compartment above that of the ECM cans where,

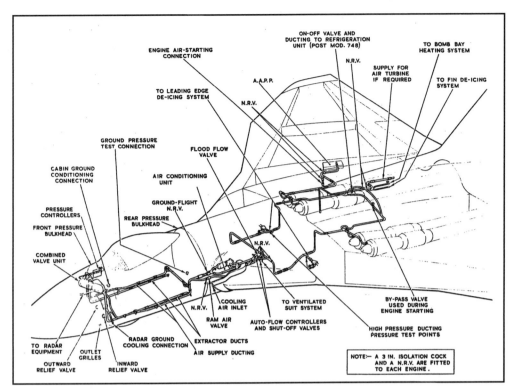

ON-OFF VALVE AND
DUCTING TO REFRIGERATION
UNIT (POST MOD. 748)

ENGINE AIR-STARTING
CONNECTION

N.R.V.

A.A.P.P.

N.R.V.

SUPPLY FOR
AIR TURBINE
IF REQUIRED

TO BOMB BAY
HEATING SYSTEM

TO FIN DE-ICING
SYSTEM

TO LEADING EDGE
DE-ICING SYSTEM

GROUND PRESSURE
TEST CONNECTION

FLOOD FLOW
VALVE

CABIN GROUND
CONDITIONING
CONNECTION

AIR CONDITIONING
UNIT

PRESSURE
CONTROLLERS

GROUND-FLIGHT
N.R.V.

FRONT PRESSURE
BULKHEAD

REAR PRESSURE
BULKHEAD

COMBINED
VALVE UNIT

N.R.V.

BY-PASS VALVE
USED DURING
ENGINE STARTING

HIGH PRESSURE DUCTING
PRESSURE TEST POINTS

COOLING
AIR INLET

TO VENTILATED
SUIT SYSTEM

N.R.V.

RAM AIR
VALVE

TO RADAR
EQUIPMENT

OUTLET
GRILLES

RADAR GROUND
COOLING CONNECTION

EXTRACTOR DUCTS

AUTO-FLOW CONTROLLERS
AND SHUT-OFF VALVES

OUTWARD
RELIEF VALVE

INWARD
RELIEF VALVE

AIR SUPPLY DUCTING

NOTE:— A 3 IN. ISOLATION COCK
AND A N.R.V. ARE FITTED
TO EACH ENGINE.

The conditioning system encompassed not only services, including pressurisation, to the cockpit, but also acted upon the engines, intakes, wings, bomb bay, and fin providing de-icing and anti-icing as required. (HSA Bitteswell)

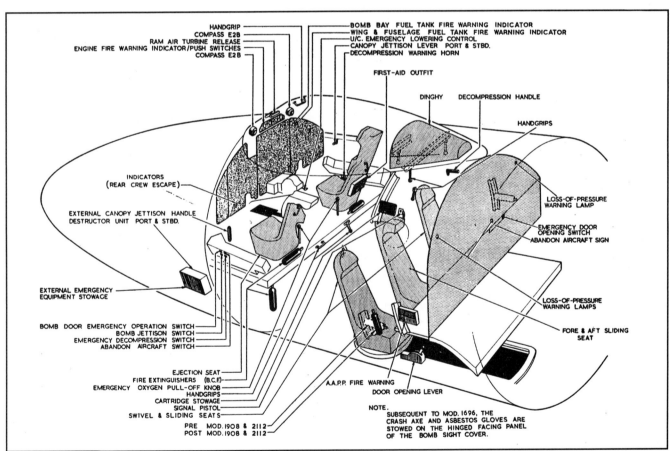

HANDGRIP
COMPASS E2B
RAM AIR TURBINE RELEASE
ENGINE FIRE WARNING INDICATOR/PUSH SWITCHES
COMPASS E2B

BOMB BAY FUEL TANK FIRE WARNING INDICATOR
WING & FUSELAGE FUEL TANK FIRE WARNING INDICATOR
U/C. EMERGENCY LOWERING CONTROL
CANOPY JETTISON LEVER PORT & STBD.
DECOMPRESSION WARNING HORN

FIRST-AID OUTFIT

DINGHY   DECOMPRESSION HANDLE

HANDGRIPS

INDICATORS
(REAR CREW ESCAPE)

LOSS-OF-PRESSURE
WARNING LAMP

EXTERNAL CANOPY JETTISON HANDLE
DESTRUCTOR UNIT PORT & STBD.

EMERGENCY DOOR
OPENING SWITCH
ABANDON AIRCRAFT SIGN

EXTERNAL EMERGENCY
EQUIPMENT STOWAGE

LOSS-OF-PRESSURE
WARNING LAMPS

BOMB DOOR EMERGENCY OPERATION SWITCH
BOMB JETTISON SWITCH
EMERGENCY DECOMPRESSION SWITCH
ABANDON AIRCRAFT SWITCH

FORE & AFT SLIDING
SEAT

EJECTION SEAT
FIRE EXTINGUISHERS (B.C.F.)
EMERGENCY OXYGEN PULL-OFF KNOB
HANDGRIPS
CARTRIDGE STOWAGE
SIGNAL PISTOL
SWIVEL & SLIDING SEATS
PRE MOD.1908 & 2112
POST MOD.1908 & 2112

A.A.P.P. FIRE WARNING

DOOR OPENING LEVER

NOTE.
SUBSEQUENT TO MOD.1696, THE
CRASH AXE AND ASBESTOS GLOVES ARE
STOWED ON THE HINGED FACING PANEL
OF THE BOMB SIGHT COVER.

The Vulcan cockpit was well equipped to take care of fire, injury, and escape depending upon the circumstances. One item not shown is the flak blanket which could be used to cover a hole in the cockpit structure thus allowing combat pressurisation to be maintained. It was normally stowed with the first aid kit. (HSA Bitteswell)

WARBIRD**TECH**
S E R I E S

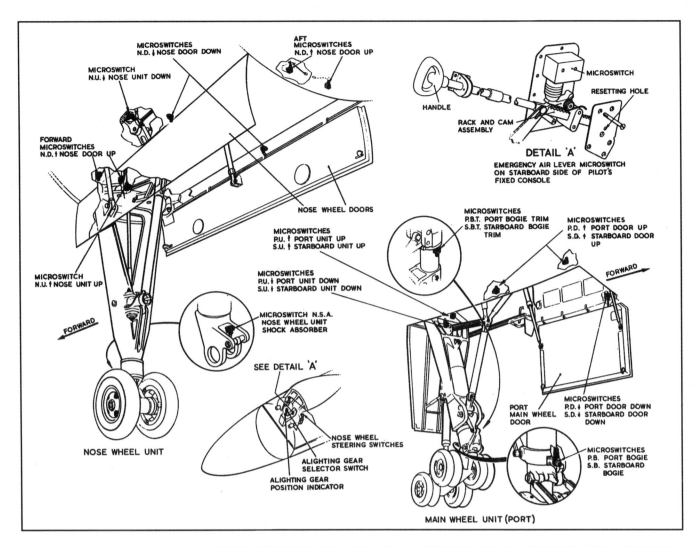

MICROSWITCHES
N.D. ↓ NOSE DOOR DOWN

MICROSWITCH
N.U. ↓ NOSE UNIT DOWN

AFT
MICROSWITCHES
N.D. ↑ NOSE DOOR UP

FORWARD
MICROSWITCHES
N.D. ↑ NOSE DOOR UP

MICROSWITCH
N.U. ↑ NOSE UNIT UP

FORWARD

NOSE WHEEL UNIT

NOSE WHEEL DOORS

MICROSWITCHES
P.U. ↑ PORT UNIT UP
S.U. ↑ STARBOARD UNIT UP

MICROSWITCHES
P.U. ↓ PORT UNIT DOWN
S.U. ↓ STARBOARD UNIT DOWN

MICROSWITCH N.S.A.
NOSE WHEEL UNIT
SHOCK ABSORBER

SEE DETAIL 'A'

NOSE WHEEL
STEERING SWITCHES

ALIGHTING GEAR
SELECTOR SWITCH

ALIGHTING GEAR
POSITION INDICATOR

HANDLE

RACK AND CAM
ASSEMBLY

MICROSWITCH

RESETTING HOLE

DETAIL 'A'
EMERGENCY AIR LEVER MICROSWITCH
ON STARBOARD SIDE OF PILOT'S
FIXED CONSOLE

MICROSWITCHES
P.B.T. PORT BOGIE TRIM
S.B.T. STARBOARD BOGIE
TRIM

MICROSWITCHES
P.D. ↑ PORT DOOR UP
S.D. ↑ STARBOARD DOOR
UP

FORWARD

PORT
MAIN WHEEL
DOOR

MICROSWITCHES
P.D. ↓ PORT DOOR DOWN
S.D. ↓ STARBOARD DOOR
DOWN

MICROSWITCHES
P.B. PORT BOGIE
S.B. STARBOARD
BOGIE

MAIN WHEEL UNIT (PORT)

Under normal circumstances the Vulcan used normal hydraulics to lower its undercarriage, however for emergency use a pneumatic blowdown system was installed which was operated by a single handle in the cockpit. (HSA Bitteswell)

Both the Vulcan B.1A and B.2 were equipped with ECM systems housed in the bulged rear fuselage. This is the B.2 as it includes the X band power unit and transmitter. Also shown is the cooling system layout and VCCP. (HSA Bitteswell)

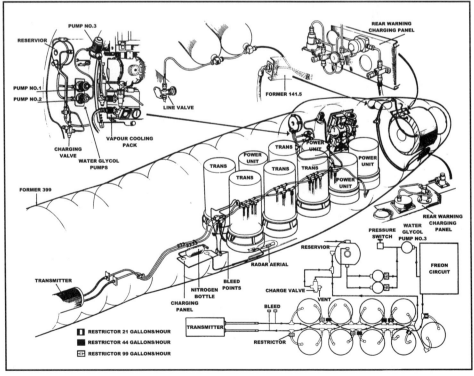

RESERVOIR

PUMP NO.3

PUMP NO.1
PUMP NO.2

CHARGING
VALVE

WATER GLYCOL
PUMPS

VAPOUR COOLING
PACK

LINE VALVE

FORMER 399

REAR WARNING
CHARGING PANEL

FORMER 141.5

POWER
UNIT

TRANS

TRANS

TRANS

TRANS

TRANS

POWER
UNIT

TRANS

TRANS

POWER
UNIT

POWER
UNIT

REAR WARNING
CHARGING
PANEL

PRESSURE
SWITCH

WATER
GLYCOL
PUMP NO.3

FREON
CIRCUIT

RESERVIOR

CHARGE VALVE

VENT

TRANSMITTER

RADAR AERIAL

NITROGEN
BOTTLE

CHARGING
PANEL

BLEED
POINTS

TRANSMITTER

BLEED

RESTRICTOR

RESTRICTOR 21 GALLONS/HOUR
RESTRICTOR 44 GALLONS/HOUR
RESTRICTOR 99 GALLONS/HOUR

Preparing for flight are the crew of XL445. Clearly visible in this view is the nose wheel steering jack at the back of the leg. The small blister between the entrance door and the wheel bay is the lower head for the periscope. This was located at the AEO's position and also had a facility for viewing the upper surfaces. (John Nickolls)

upon deployment, it acted straight down the Vulcan's centreline – not slightly offset as had previously been the case. The only visible evidence of an ECM fit appeared on a flat, blended in, counterpoise panel that was bolted onto the rear section of the starboard jet pipe structures. This feature appeared on both the Vulcan B.1A and B.2 whilst those optimised for Blue Steel carriage also had another plate fitted on the port side jet pipe tunnels. Aerials on these plates were in the main unobtrusive – the two forward positions being retained for a pair of noise jamming Red Shrimp domes whilst the third slot on the plate normally had a blade aerial showing for the "L" band jammer.

Other detection and suppression systems fitted to the Vulcan included Blue Saga "S" band whose small dipoles appeared as barely visible bumps on the nose. The H2S radar also received a very useful modification known as Fishpond which enabled the Nav Rad to use the system to detect incoming aircraft from in front and below within the compass of the scanner sweep. As Soviet radar technology improved,

The crew entrance door has a removable ladder which allows the door to be used as an escape chute in an emergency by the rear crew. Leading up from the door is the ladder that gives access to the flight deck. The door normally used pneumatics for retraction, however in an emergency a blowdown system would be operated which would force the door into the airflow and lock it into position. Normal opening was by gravity although if the door vent iced up, which happened occasionally, other sometimes dubious means had to be used to let the crew out. (Damien Burke)

further upgrades were added to the Vulcan's repertoire. One of the most useful was the "X" band system which could jam the radars of Soviet fighters. This brought the total of offensive avionics systems in the rear fuselage up to five. Only the "X" band power unit was locat-

ed with the others, the jammer itself occupied the position in the lower rear fuselage once destined for the motor portion of the Blue Steel missile. Not all defensive electronics need to generate a signal to be effective. This was the premise behind the ARI 18228 radar warn-

These gaping bomb doors reveal a wealth of detail to the practised eye. On the lower section of the front bulkhead/wing spar, the cutout for the Blue Steel can clearly be seen. Peeking out below the support beam are the door operating jacks – each pair is operated by a separate sequence valve, when they go out of synch the effect is quite destructive. (BBA Collection)

On the rear bulkhead also are located a pair of operating jacks and a slightly less obtrusive fairing and cutout for the Blue Steel missile. The pipework in the roof provides de-ice and anti-ice and heating services to the bomb bay and the fin. The two runs of pipework just above the bomb door are (from the bottom) the fuel gallery and above it the spraybars for the bomb bay extinguishers. (BBA Collection)

ing receiver which appeared on many RAF aircraft during the early 1970s. In the Vulcan's case, trials began using XM597 in 1972, the system known as Green Butter, being cleared for widespread service use in 1973.

All this new equipment fitted to the Vulcan meant that the AEO and his increasing workload finally came into his own. Not only was the aircraft power management, both normal and emergency within his purview, so was the control of the defensive electronics. During peacetime the power hungry ECM cans were identified as non-essential electrical items within the context of an emergency, however in wartime things would have changed with the systems being switched to the primary position in front of all the navigation and bombing systems. Even the latter underwent some augmentation when the SFOM bomb sight began to appear on the copilot's coaming from the mid 1970s. Using the tip of the aircraft's refuel probe for calibration, the reticule gunsight enabled the aircraft to carry out high speed low level laydown attacks using retarded 1,000 lbs. bombs or to manually line up and release a nuclear weapon over a target.

The appearance of the Valiant, Victor, and Vulcan into the service of Bomber Command had given rise to the use of the sobriquet "V Force" to describe all three types collectively. Such a change in the technology presented to Bomber Command had led to the creation of a whole training infrastructure to support the needs of the squadrons. The

ed in racking within the fuselage which also housed the pupils and their instructors. On first formation the unit was known as the BCBS which later changed to the SCBS upon the creation of Strike Command. Throughout its life however the school was invariably irreverently known as 1066 Sqdn.

Flight testing of the new rear fuselage was entrusted to the third production Vulcan B.2, XH534, which first flew in this new configuration in 1959. Controller (Aircraft) flying occupied this Vulcan throughout the remainder of 1959 and well into 1960. Operating from A&AEE Boscombe Down the assigned Vulcan B.2s cleared the type for squadron service in May 1960. On 1 July the first delivery, XH558, to 230 OCU was undertaken.

The first unit to equip with the Vulcan B.2 was No.83 Sqdn which had been reduced to a B.1 cadre at Waddington on 10 August 1960 before reappearing at Scampton on 10 October in its new guise. It was soon joined by the newly recreated 27 Sqdn which reformed on 1 April 1961. The final B.2 unit at Scampton was 617 Sqdn which began to hand its previous B.1As to 50 Sqdn at Waddington from 1 September. With 88 airframes on order, although only 87 were delivered as one aircraft —XM596 – was never completed and remained at Chatterton for use as a fatigue test specimen, the opportunity was afforded the RAF to create another bomber wing. Located at RAF Coningsby, Lincolnshire, the first resident unit was 9 Sqdn which reformed on 1 March 1962. Four months later on 1 July, No.12 Sqdn came into existence as a Vulcan B.2 operator having previously had Canberras on its inventory.

The 6th (and opposite placed 7th) seat in the Vulcan was added as an afterthought squeezed as it was between the rear crew floor and the bomb aimer's position. From personal experience the author can vouch for the fact that it was cold and uncomfortable. The ladder on the left leads to the flight deck. This ladder would have to be slid sideways whenever a VIP bed was fitted in the bomb aimer's position. (Mel James)

most visible aspect of this process was the appearance of the HP Hastings T.5 which were a handful of transports converted to act as flying classrooms for the airborne training of navigators in the use of the H2S system. To aid in this process, a scanner was located in a radome under the aircraft's centre section whilst the relevant black boxes were locat-

With its bomb doors open to show the front drum fuel tank, this Vulcan B.2 overflies Akrotiri. Of note are the plethora of suppressed aerials clustered about the nose gear bay. The largest of these housed the Rad Alt Mk6. Also clearly visible are the complex cambers involved in creating the wing leading edge. (John Nickolls)

The level of expertise within the Vulcan force was such that Bomber Command were more than happy to accept an invitation from USAF to participate in "Exercise Skyshield" whose sole aim was to test the NORAD defence system to its fullest extent. Eight Vulcan B.2s from the Scampton Wing participated, attacking various targets after the main force of SAC bombers, B-47s, B-52s, and supporting EB-57s, had already penetrated

the net. Split into two groups of four, one from the north and one from the south, the delta bombers not only managed to successfully penetrate the defensive radar shield undetected, but those fighters that were encountered were completely outflown by the combination of height and speed.

During this period, the Vulcan B.2 was cleared to operate with a number of nuclear weapons including

Blue Danube and the smaller American controlled devices. However Soviet air defence technology was advancing quite rapidly at this point and it was soon recognised that the days of high altitude attacks carried out with impunity were soon to be a thing of the past.

All was not lost as the development of a far more potent weapon was already taking place – the Avro Blue Steel stand-off missile.

Normally shrouded by a dull grey casing this shot reveals the Red Steer TWR in all its detail. Those used to the Meteor night fighter would be familiar with this equipment. (Damien Burke)

Ground crew fit a replacement TBC to the bay of XH558. By this time a winch was being used to close the bay door and this can be seen hanging underneath the aircraft. Plugged into the starboard wing just aft of the gear bay is the hose from the Palouste air starting unit. (BBA Collection)

WARBIRDTECH
S E R I E S

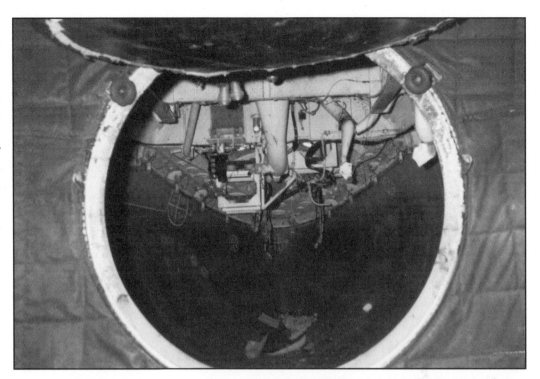

This raised flap gives access from the cockpit to the radome for ground servicing purposes. The substantial nose longerons that supported the weight of the radome can clearly be seen. In this view the H2S scanner has been removed. (BBA Collection)

Sitting forlorn at St. Athan prior to scrapping, Vulcan B.2 XM650 is minus its nose beak and radome. This reveals details not normally visible such as the access hatch to the radar scanner in the front bulkhead. Also visible above the hatch is the tank for the bomb aimer's screen de-icing fluid. The bellows connections for the in-flight refuelling system are also noticeable as is the inwards/outwards relief valve for the cabin pressurisation system. (BBA Collection)

Peeking over the shoulder of the AEO reveals the plethora of switches, dials, and knobs facing each rear crew member. The small porthole was for daylight purposes only. Close to it was housed an emergency Verey flare pistol and its cartridge container. The striped cover by the AEO's knee hides the entrance door electrical release. (Mel James)

This view of the "coalmine" reveals the equipment at the Nav Plotters position – much of it associated with the arcane art of navigation although some of the Nav Radars equipment did intrude. Just showing on the left is the screen for the NBS system which rejoiced in the name of the the indicator – wave guide generator. In fact these were two separate pieces of equipment that were matched as a pair in the avionics bay. (Damien Burke)

This on high shot of the Vulcans of 83 Sqdn lined up for an inspection reveals the suppressed aerials in the upper fuselage and dorsal fairing. Located at the base of the fin is the fibreglass cover for the Collins ADF. (BAe/Avro Heritage)

Handley Page Hastings TG529 was converted to T.5 standard to train navigators in the intricacies of the NBS radar in an airborne environment. The system scanner is in the radome under the fuselage whilst all the black boxes are housed inside the fuselage in racking. (C. P. Russell-Smith Collection)

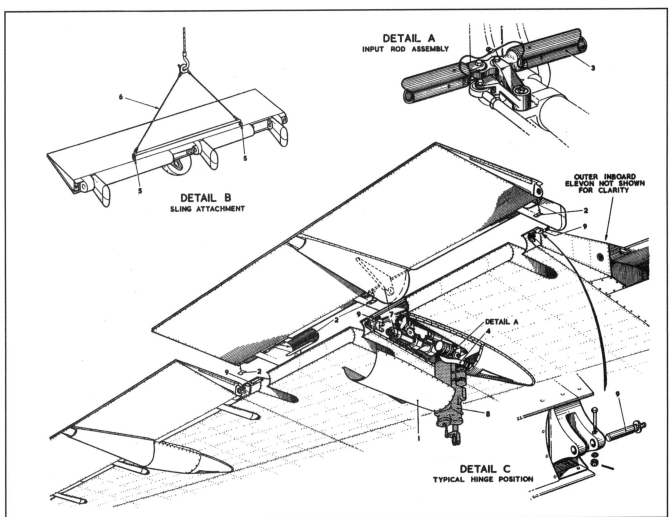

Due to the refinement of the Vulcan's outer wings during the implementation of the Phase2C wing, the outboard PFCUs had to be housed in raised fairings below the wings. (NATO AM)

WARBIRD**TECH** SERIES

On a flyby practising asymmetric handling is B.2 XH537 – note the rudder deflection. This aircraft was originally allocated for Skybolt clearance trials before joining the RAF. Seen in the unloaded trailing position are the mainwheel bogies with the jacks above at full extension. (C. P. Russell-Smith Collection)

Overseas Ranger flights were part and parcel of life for the Vulcan fleet. Depending on the duration and the requirements of the trip a bomb bay pannier of the relevant size would be required. That to the side of XL360 is of the 4,000 lbs. variety. Into this would be packed spare wheels, a TBC, tools, a small technical library, the crew's kit, and any other required items. (Mel James)

This view of B.2 XH534 reveals many of the undersurface details. At the front of the engine bays are the heat exchangers for the oil cooling and lubrication system. To the rear are the vents for the ram air that has cooled the engines and jet pipes. The small blister under the tip of the rear fuselage is the tail bumper which was connected via a microswitch to a warning light in the cockpit. (C. P. Russell-Smith Collection)

This line up of Vulcans on the ORP at Finningley in 1964 are awaiting crews for a scramble. All sport gloss white undersurfaces which indicates that they are optimised for the low level free fall role. (C. P. Russell-Smith Collection)

One of the lesser known requirements exercised by a landing aircraft is the deployment of the landing lights visible here under the wings as small black shapes. This Vulcan was one of those that was required to carry the Blue Steel missile therefore two counterpoise panels are carried. (C. P. Russell-Smith Collection)

Complete with TFR pod and flight refuelling probe B.2 XM574 prepares to touch down at Luqa, Malta. The angle of approach was quite normal for the Vulcan, however when using aerodynamic braking the nose was pulled up even further. (C. P. Russell-Smith Collection)

This nose on view of a Vulcan being marshalled into its slot reveals many details of this Cyprus based machine. On the starboard jet pipe tunnels is the counterpoise panel upon which the ECM aerials are mounted. The visible aerial is the "L" band just forward of which would be the two dimples associated with the Red Shrimp jammers. (John Nickolls)

Vulcan B.2 XH560 taxies into its slot at Akrotiri after a sortie. Clearly visible under the wings outboard of the main gear bay are the mounts for the defunct Skybolt system. The large blade aerial visible under the rear fuselage is the "L" band ECM aerial. On the original colour print the anticollision beacons can clearly be seen. (John Nickolls)

Avro Vulcan B.2XH539 spent its working life as a development aircraft with the MoA and the A&AEE. The pattern of black marks on the bomb bay doors was used for calibration tracking of ballistic drops. To record these events, cameras were fitted in housings on the wingtips and under the lower fuselage. Of note is the fin badge which is that of the AFSC. (C. P. Russell-Smith Collection)

Sat on its ORP finger, Vulcan B.2 XL425 is prepared for flight. Visible are a set of air cylinders charging up the door emergency system, a CO2 fire trolley, and a 28v DC/200v AC power unit whose cables are plugged into the rear fuselage. The very thin cable evident is the connection between the ASC and the crew. (C. P. Russell-Smith Collection)

With intake blanks fitted to keep out the birds and the rain, B.2 XH562 of 35 Sqdn also has a 28vDC power supply plugged into the auxiliary power supply point by the nosewheel doors. (C. P. Russell-Smith Collection)

The second production Vulcan B.2, XH534, was used for type clearance trials by the manufacturers and the C(A). The fin badge is that of Avro. (C. P. Russell-Smith Collection)

To gain access to the cockpit windows for cleaning and the application of rain repellent, an item of AGE called a giraffe was required. This Vulcan B.2 XL427 represents the type as delivered and is allocated to 83 Sqdn. (C. P. Russell-Smith Collection)

BOMBING COLOUR

The colour schemes worn by the various marques of Vulcan have always reflected their particular role at a certain point of their career. A vital precursor was shown by the prototypes, both of which appeared in gleaming gloss white. However initial deliveries to the RAF wore an overall silver scheme, though this soon changed to the more familiar white which was referred to as an anti flash finish. Both B.1's and the later B.2 variants wore this scheme which was only lightened by the various pale coloured anti flash marking applied. This persisted until it was realised that Soviet air defences had improved, such that a change of emphasis was required. Thus attack and strike roles were to be flown at low level. To reflect this change in policy the Vulcans acquired grey green upper surfaces albeit still gloss. In the 1970's the requirement for a gloss finish disappeared and was replaced by an overall matt covering. Originally this was two greys and a green highlighted by two colour roundels and fin flashes. Further splashes of colour emerged when operating units became semi-autonomous in 1975 and squadron markings were applied. Some gloss work was still retained on the Vulcans of 27 Squadron whose role of fallout sampling required that the airframe retain a smooth gloss finish although low viz national marking were still retained. A further change required that the lower surfaces of the Operation Corporate Vulcans were painted dark instead of light grey. The final touch was to the K.2 tankers which gained an inverted "T" painted in white under the belly. This was set off by black and dayglo guidelines for receiver aircraft. Special markings have also been seen on the type-at least one bomber had a Playboy Bunny fin badge whilst those aircraft taking part in the 1977 SAC Giant Voice Competition returned home bedecked in Queens Silver Jubilee markings and the SAC sash and 2.BW badges on the nose.

Photographed from the Meteor T7 chase plane, Vulcan B1 XA895 on the strength of 230 OCU, Waddington, is finished in overall silver with black highlights. The fin badge is that of the City of Lincoln and was worn by Waddington aircraft only. (BAe/Avro Heritage)

Armed with a pair of aerodynamic Skybolt test rounds, Vulcan XH537 is fully equipped with fairings on the wingtips and the centre lower fuselage. These housed cameras that recorded every move of the missiles as they cleared the aircraft. Of note is the truncated flight refuelling probe. (BAe/Avro Heritage)

Wearing "Giant Voice" exercise markings is B2 XH538 pictured at Waddington on pan Delta 13. By this time the 1 Group Panthers head had gravitated from the fuselage to the fin. (Mel James)

The primary trials vehicle for the FSD versions of Blue Steel was Vulcan B.1 XA903. On this aircraft the weapon was only partly recessed into the belly unlike those Vulcans that carried the live rounds. The markings on the missile are red and white, this aiding the ballistic recording cameras to track the vehicle accurately after it leaves the carrier. (BAe/Avro Heritage)

Lifting off from Woodford on a test flight is this Vulcan K2 which reveals the extent of the white painted areas needed to help incoming aircraft line up correctly on the black and dayglo guidelines. (BAe/Avro Heritage)

High above Oakham the capital of Rutland, Vulcan XH558 has just flown past RAF Cottesmore in a farewell flypast. The delicate blending of the wings and fuselage still hold true to the early ideas formatted by Roy Chadwick. (Bob Archer)

The only Vulcan to be the subject of questions in the Houses of Parliament is the now preserved XH558 which was grounded reportedly due to lack of funds. In its long career the Vulcan served as a B.2, B.2 (MRR), and a K.2. (Bob Archer)

BLUE STEEL AND SKYBOLT

I n its early days the "V" force was intended for use at high level in either the nuclear strike freefall or conventional attack roles. All the intended targets were within the bounds of the Soviet Union and other countries deemed as threats within the Warsaw Pact. Although this list is still classified as secret, it is suspected of including airfields, radar complexes, and SAM sites.

However Soviet defensive tactics and awareness had increased to such a level that conventional overflight tactics became less and less of a viable option that they bordered almost on the suicidal. The solution to the problem of hitting such targets whilst retaining the services of the carrier aircraft came for the RAF in the shape of the Blue Steel standoff missile. Realising full well that the Soviet air defence network would never remain static, planning for such a weapon had begun tentatively in 1954 as a combined effort between Avro and the RAE.

Although it was possible to theorize much of the required design, the lack of computer technology meant that at some stage the missile had to leave the laboratory to be tried in the real world. Therefore in 1955, the decision was taken to build two freeflight aerodynamic test vehicles. This step would also allow the creation of a proving trials organisation to develop the in service weapon. In March 1956, the MoS issued design and development contracts to Avro for overall design leadership whilst Armstrong Whitworth were charged with

building the propulsion motors. The avionics firm Elliot Brothers in conjunction with the RAE became responsible for the INS, a great technological leap in that era. DeHavilland Aircraft's missile division also became involved being contracted to provide the vehicle's power supply turbines. Armament was the sole responsibility of the RAE. By 1957, enough design work had been completed to allow the joint trials team to take over.

The first Blue Steel trials vehicles were built to 2/3rd scale and were air launched from a Vickers Valiant bomber based at the Avro weapons research division, Woodford. Carried internally within the bomb bay the test launches were

carried out over the Aberporth range on the coast of Wales. Dropped initially as a conventional ballistic weapon the model would be clear of the carrier before the solid fuel motor fired. At this stage in development only a simple autopilot was available for control, therefore flight time was limited to minutes before it was necessary to press the destruct button. Throughout 1958 and the early months of 1959, aerodynamic and performance trials of the scale missiles continued allowing the design team to incorporate any refinements or corrections that were required. In the later stages of the drop trials testbed Vulcan B.1 XA903 also became involved giving all involved some idea of how

Lifting off from the Woodford runway trials Vulcan XA903 with an aerodynamic trials missile as the underslung load. A camera fairing has been installed behind the bomb aimer's blister to record the separation of missile from aircraft. (BAe/Avro Heritage)

After their service with the RAF some discarded Blue Steel rounds suitably disarmed were retained for preservation purposes. With its lower folding fin fully deployed is this example at Newark, Notts. (BBA Collection)

the full scale article might behave when launched from one of the intended carrier aircraft types. The next stage was to construct test articles of the full scale Blue Steel. Primary construction material was intended to be stainless steel thus emulating that of the in service weapon, however problems with manufacture meant that early examples of the FSD missiles were constructed of aluminum instead. In place of the intended A.W. Stentor engine which was still in development, a substitute powerplant from DeHavilland guided missile division, namely the Double Spectre, was used instead. As this part of the programme had been running in parallel with the smaller scale powered missile tests, the first full scale unpowered dummies were ready for trial drops over the Aberporth range in late 1958. Powered aerodynamic trials of the FSD missiles began over the Woomera test range in Australia in 1959 and were to continue throughout 1960. As well as flight behaviour of the missile, various other phases of the carrier and launch regime were also explored. Important questions

were answered during this period. How would the missile behave at minus temperatures at high altitude? Would problems occur during the launch and subsequent supersonic flight? In both these areas the Blue Steel came through with flying colours. In fact, only one part of the whole process gave some cause for concern, that being the interface between the missile and the carrier aircraft.

This particular niggle was to plague the missile throughout its operational life and often resulted in hard pressed ground crews juggling aircraft and missiles in an attempt to find compatible pairings. Once successfully mated it was not unknown for the Nav Rad to use the missile INS system to update the bombers NBS, such was the systems accuracy.

Eventually all the manufacturing problems were overcome and the first FSD stainless steel missiles were declared for evaluation. In the summer of 1960 at Woomera, Vulcan B.1 XA903 began the final run of testing and evaluation of the

missile. One change from the earlier trial Blue Steels was the fitment of the A.W. Stentor rocket engine which brought these pre-production FSDs close to fully operational standard. The primary usage for these vehicles covered the behaviour of the onboard INS plus the missile guidance control system. During this period, XA903 was joined in the trials programme by Vulcan B.2 XH539 which was the prime FSD carrier over the Woomera ranges throughout 1961. Concurrent with the development of the weapon came the design of the transporter vehicles required for its carriage and the test equipment required to clear the missile for fitment to an aircraft. As the Blue Steel was destined for carriage under both the Victor and Vulcan, a common set of interfaces was developed that covered the release mechanism, hydraulics, power supplies, cooling and heating, electrical control, and of course, the bugbear of the whole programme, the monitoring, data, and lanyard operating plugs. These consisted of 157 surface to surface contacts instead of pins that ensured a clean separa-

To house the Blue Steel under the Vulcan, a special fairing was manufactured the only moving parts of which were the fin gap doors. Not only were all the connectors housed on this assemble, so were many of the services needed to operate the weapon. (NATO AM)

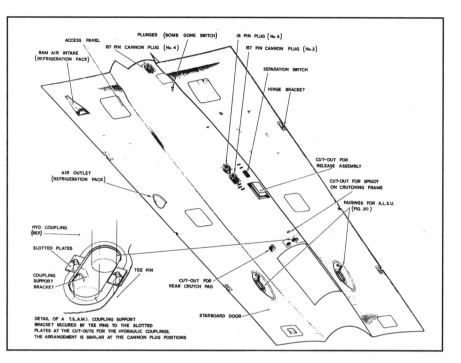

tion upon launch. Although contact between these interfaces worked most times under test conditions, under operational squadron usage the scene was often different as frustrated armourers moved from aircraft to aircraft trying to find a pair that could read each other correctly. One other vital piece of equipment developed and

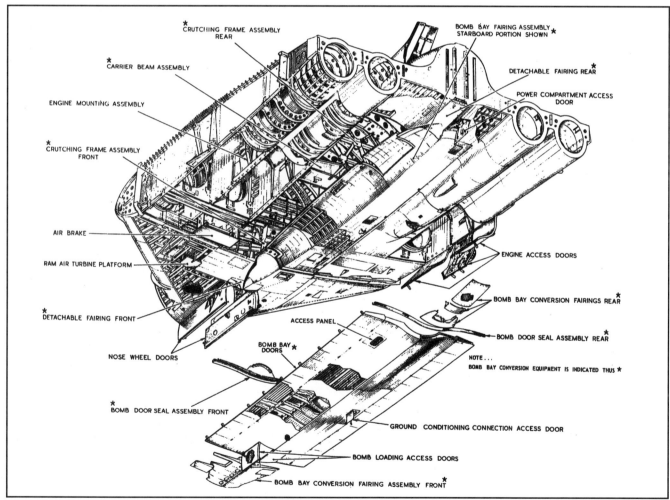

Both sets of bomb doors plus associated fairings are illustrated here. As modifications were embodied on the Blue Steel aircraft, so it became increasingly difficult to change roles between free-fall and stand-off carrier. (NATO AM)

Overshooting its home base, Blue Steel equipped Vulcan B.2 XL443 reveals the missile's lower fin in the stowed or landing position. The upper fin was surrounded by the fin gap doors which were connected to the suitably relabelled bomb door switch at the captain's position. This aircraft is unusual in that it carries three Red Shrimp domes on the starboard counterpoise panel instead of the usual two. (C. P. Russell-Smith Collection)

deployed in support of the Blue Steel missile was the much needed water bath. This was required for immediate immersion of any person splashed by the rocket's propellant Hydrogen Peroxide. To give its correct and full name High Test Peroxide works in conjunction with the other fuel carried by the missile, that being kerosene. As a carbon fuel finds it difficult to burn at altitude, the HTP provides the required chemical mix to allow the fuel to burn at great heat and power under any circumstances. The down side of this is that HTP is very dangerous and needs to be handled with clinical precision, otherwise self combustion can occur due to the high decomposition rate of the chemical.

Surrounded by the usual selection of ground support and test equipment is XL321 of 617 Sqdn. As this was a public display, it is highly likely that the underslung Blue Steel is a navigation training round. (C. P. Russell-Smith Collection)

Other equipment developed in support of the main programme included a trainer version. This aerodynamic vehicle was built without propellant tanks, engines, or armament system. It did however contain the full Blue Steel command, control, and guidance systems and was used to train crews in the operation of the missile right up to the launch point. Upon the successful completion of the trials programme, the Blue Steel stand-off missile was cleared for service usage.

Entry into Royal Air Force service began with the Vulcans of the Scampton based 617 Sqdn whose first examples arrived for deploy-

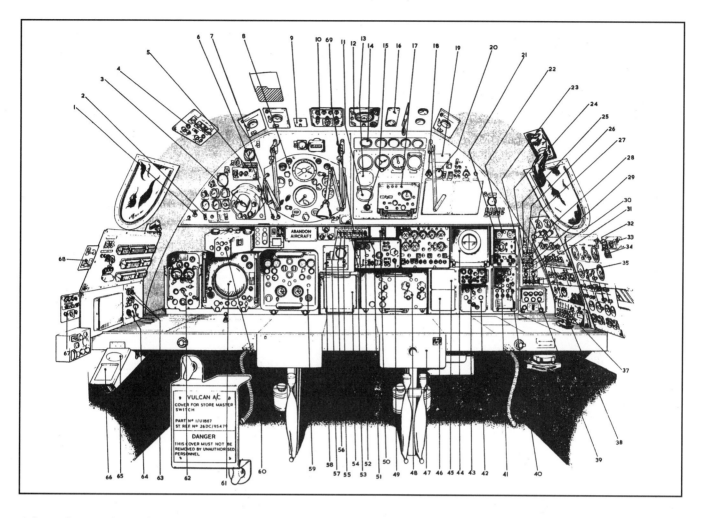

When Blue Steel was fitted some of the panels were altered at the rear crew positions. Further changes took place when Skybolt was being mooted as a Blue Steel replacement. (NATO AM)

ment during September 1962. Initial operating capability was achieved in October just in time to reach alert status because of the Cuban missile crisis. Due to the wait imposed whilst waiting for aircraft conversion kits and the need to train crews, the squadron had to wait until February 1963 before being declared fully operational. It was intended that the Vulcan could be re-roled to either conventional or Blue Steel as and when required by the use of these conversion kits which housed all the requirements for each on a bomb trolley. In practise as modification action continued, it became impractical to convert the Blue Steel carriers between roles thus those fitted normally

remained so. It was during this time that the designation of B.2A was sometimes used to identify such aircraft, however an alternative was also used this being B.2(BS). Later in the Vulcan's career, the B.2A designation was frequently applied to those aircraft powered by Olympus 301 ECUs. One of the major alterations carried out on the airframe to accommodate the Blue Steel was modification 200 which called for a semi circular cutout to be applied to the lower part of the front and rear spars to clear the weapon. Most aircraft were built with this modification – those that had been released for service earlier were modified retrospectively by their units. Extra curricular training on

the missile and its systems was presented as part of the Blue Steel course that was held at RAF Lindholme home of the BCBS. With No. 617 Sqdn successfully converted to the Blue Steel it was the turn of the two other Scampton based squadrons to follow suit. In late 1963, Nos. 27 and 83 Squadrons were declared operationally ready.

The appearance of the Blue Steel in the inventory also brought about a revision in operating procedures. Unlike Strategic Air Command, the RAF had neither the money or resources to keep a deterrent force airborne 24 hours a day. Thus the ORP at the end of the runway came into being. Alert status, known as

QRA, kept crews and their aircraft on standby 365 days a year. Coupled with the introduction of the rapid air start system for the engines this meant that under alert launch procedures a flight of four Vulcans could be airborne in under two minutes. The rapid air system consisted of a series of high pressure air bottles which could hold a maximum charge of 3,300 psi. Upon selection on engine start, a blast of high pressure air rushed though the starter unit bringing the Olympus engine to life. Thus the Vulcan became truly independent whilst on deployment. One feature of the Vulcan B.2 that was never used in service was the JATO rocket assisted launcher whose mounts were located just aft of each engine pairing between the jet pipes and also contained the charging point for the rapid start system. Blue Steel remained in front-line operational service until the task of maintaining Britain's nuclear deterrent passed to the submarines of the Royal Navy on 30 June 1969.

Even as Blue Steel was entering its test and development phase news from the United States began to excite interest within the senior ranks of Bomber Command. In a similar fashion to the RAF, Strategic Air Command had progressed to the point where they too were capable of carrying nuclear tipped missiles under the wings of their prime strategic bomber the B-52. The weapon in question was the GAM-77/AGM-28 Hound Dog which was regarded as an interim weapon prior to the introduction of something with more destructive power. This was the developing Douglas XGM-87A Skybolt which was proposed for carriage by the Boeing B-52 and the Convair B-58 Hustler. Part of weapons system WS-138A the 38 ft. long Skybolt was designed as an ALBM capable of supersonic speeds up to Mach 9.0 with a range of 1,150 miles.

British interest was first aroused in 1959 when details of the new weapon were released. Seen as a replacement for Blue Steel it would have extended the RAF airborne deterrent role until the mid 1970s at least. After negotiations between Premier Harold Macmillan and President Dwight D. Eisenhower at Camp David in March 1960, a deal was struck that would eventually see 100 Douglas Skybolts being delivered to the RAF. From the outset Avro and its Vulcan were seen as the prime contractor and launch platform respectively. Handley Page, builders of the Victor, also expressed an interest in providing their aircraft as a carrier. However this option was soon rejected as the low ground clearance of the Victor was considered insurmountable especially for a multi-finned missile such as the Skybolt.

To reinforce Avro's premier role in the introduction of the Skybolt, Vulcan B.2s currently under construction at Chatterton began to receive the necessary under wing hardpoints and associated services starting with the fortieth aircraft.

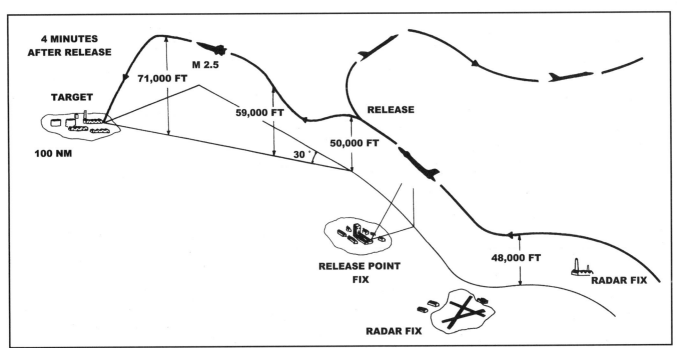

This diagram illustrates the hi-level profile adopted by the "V" force when launching Blue Steel. (BBA Collection)

Not all Vulcan B.2s were allocated to the stand-off missile attack role. XJ781 of 12 Sqdn was one of the aircraft that retained a conventional as well as a nuclear free-fall role. (Ray Deacon)

Other modifications included localised airframe structural strengthening and the installation of Olympus series 301 ECUs rated at 20,000 lbs. st. each. The trials aircraft allocated to the Olympus programme was Vulcan B.2 XH557. Flying from Filton, Bristol, the bomber also airtested a pair of Olympus 22R engines in the Nos. 1 and 4 positions. This latter powerplant was intended for the ill-fated, but technically excellent TSR-2. For three years this particular aircraft was employed as an engine test bed before being returned to normal build standard and delivery to the Royal Air Force.

Two other Vulcans were employed on trials connected with the Skybolt programme. Both were bailed to the MoS prior to entering RAF service, thus XH537 in company with XH538 were involved with the missile proving trials. An earlier excursion to the Douglas factory, Santa Monica, by Vulcan XH563 in

Caught at the point of liftoff is Vulcan B.2 XL390 of 617 Sqdn which has received the TFR pod in the nose tip and a flight refuelling probe. By this time the standard ECM aerial fit of two Red Shrimps and an L band aerial was fitted. This arrangement barely changed in the following ten years. (C. P. Russell-Smith Collection)

When the Blue Steel first entered service the normal carrier aircraft was powered by series 201 ECUs, however XL390 is a series 301 ECU machine. Even as the undercarriage is retracting, the lower fin on the training round is moving to the deployed position. (C. P. Russell-Smith Collection)

1961 for electrical compatibility tests had been completed successfully thus removing one hurdle from the equation.

To enable the UK to maintain control over the missile and its possible use it was decided that a British designed warhead would be used.

This aspect of the programme was progressed at Aldermarston scene of many anti-nuclear marches in the 1960s. Whilst the warhead was being developed the Vulcan trials aircraft were carrying out aerodynamic and handling trials. In November 1961, XH537 began test flying from the Avro weapons research division airfield at Woodford with a pair of dummy Skybolt missiles underwing. By December the first test drops were being carried out over the armament trials range at West Freugh, Scotland. Both trials Vulcans eventually test dropped two missiles each with the test being filmed by cameras housed in wingtip fairings. To emulate as closely as possible proposed operating conditions, all test runs were carried out at an altitude of 45,000 ft. at an indicated airspeed of Mach 0.84. To assist with the British input into the missiles development, a joint service trials unit was established at Eglin AFB, Florida in 1962. Their duties included work within the missile programme with special interest being paid to any aspect that could cause problems for the carrier aircraft.

Although the support structure was in place and the dummy drops had been successfully achieved, development of the

By 1964, the role of the Vulcan had been changed to that of low level penetration. To reinforce the change, the upper surfaces were painted in a grey green camouflage pattern although the gloss white anti-flash paint was retained. (C. P. Russell-Smith Collection)

Complete with betraying exhaust plumes this Vulcan B.2 banks away from the camera. The folding fin of the missile is now fully deployed. As you would expect, two counterpoise panels are fitted to the jet pipe tunnels of this aircraft although the starboard one is the only one with aerials fitted. (C. P. Russell-Smith Collection)

operational weapon was running into difficulties. Problems were being encountered with both the propulsion and guidance control system. However as each successive launch later showed each problem area was being successfully addressed. By this time the programme had cost in the region of $500 million and was on increasingly shaky ground as other American ICBMs were successfully coming on line. The silo launched Minuteman missile was already entering USAF service whilst the US Navy was awaiting delivery of

the Polaris missile and its associated submarine platform. With these events in the background, it is not surprising that in November 1967 that US Secretary of State Robert McNamara recommended that the whole project be cancelled. In December the President and Premier MacMillan met in Nassau in the Bahamas to discuss the Skybolt question. From the British point of view, plans were already in an advanced state for the first test firing of a live missile from a Vulcan during 1963. As a launch platform the Vulcan had proved to

be very stable, so much so, that plans were already afoot to develop the aircraft even further with the enlarged Phase 6 wing which would be capable of carrying six such missiles. All of these plans of course counted for naught as the whole programme was cancelled as the meetings were going on. The irony is that even as the joint decision was taken a final airborne launch took place that saw the Skybolt perform as advertised.

Although the Skybolt programme was dead, the air launch idea

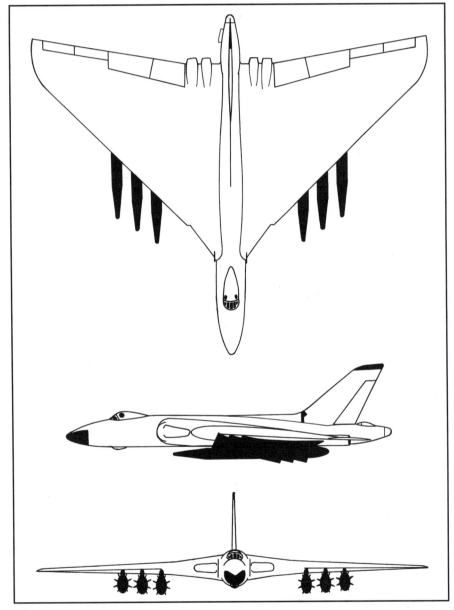

This remaining dummy Skybolt was obtained for display in the RAF Museum at Hendon after refurbishment. The amount of fins on this missile precluded their carriage by the lower slung Victor. (Mel James)

The ultimate Vulcan complete with the enlarged Phase 6 wing which was designed to lift six Skybolts aloft. (BBA Collection)

seemed to have inspired the aircraft design teams in the UK to greater aspirations. For the Vulcan this meant such strange ideas as hanging three Folland Gnat two seat trainers under the airframe. These would be armed with a nuclear warhead and flown from the drop point some 1,000 miles away by pilots who would then have the choice of ejecting from their flying bomb or perishing with the aircraft. Needless to say such a lunatic idea was soon dropped. However in 1974 during Exercise Northern Wedding, an extensive NATO exercise, Vulcans of the Waddington Wing were called upon to simulate air launched cruise missiles using Gnat trainers. These aircraft from 4 FTS were flown in formation with their allocated bomber until they reached the theoretical release point. Here the Vulcan would provide navigation and guidance data before turning away and leaving the Gnats to fly onto their targets still pretending to be cruise missiles.

VULCANS IN FULL FLIGHT

VULCANS COME – VULCANS GO

By 1964, Britain's airborne deterrent was at its zenith. In service with Bomber Command of the RAF were 43 Vickers Valiants, 32 HP Victors, and 69 Vulcans of which 45 were armed with Blue Steel stand-off weapons allocated to three squadrons. The remaining aircraft were Vulcan B.1As whose operational life was drawing to a close. This was also a time when the air defences of the USSR were improving in the areas of radar and depth of SAM deployment. So much so that the whole policy of Vulcan weapons delivery had been rethought for both the freefall and Blue Steel roles. Another factor, homegrown this time, that changed the emphasis was the ulti-

mate demise of the BAC TSR-2 which had been optimized from its inception for the high speed low level penetration role. This left the RAF without a long range interdictor, the nearest in the inventory being the EE Co. Canberra B(I)8 which in comparison was short-ranged. Thus the requirement was to be met by adapting the "V" force to the task. Of all the three "V" bombers only the Vulcan ultimately transferred to such an existence in the rougher and thicker air prevalent at such levels.

As Vulcan B.2 deliveries continued, the earlier marque slowly retired as did the Vickers Valiant which was grounded en-masse when one

landed with a massive crack in the rear wing spar. Not only had the increased flexure of the aircraft's wing at low level put paid to the airframes fatigue index, so had years of hauling large quantities of fuel in the tanker role.

The final Vulcan B.2 delivery to Bomber Command was XM657 which joined the strength of 35 Sqdn in December 1964. This last aircraft into the inventory now brought the three Vulcan bomber wings up to full strength. Located at Coningsby were the aircraft of Nos. 9, 12, and 35 Sqdns whilst Scampton housed the Blue Steel equipped 27, 83, and 617 Sqdns. The final wing was located on the

After their working lives were over, retired Vulcan airframes were used for training and instructional purposes. Once XA899 of the Bedford based BLEU this aircraft has been renumbered as 7812M in the maintenance series. The position of the flying controls occurs when the system hydraulic pressure dissipates or the solenoid valves revert to the central bypass position and the aircraft has been subject to the vagaries of the wind. (Ray Deacon)

AVRO
VULCAN

79

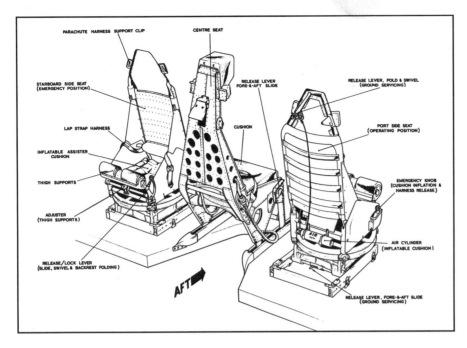

One of the most important modifications applied to the rear crew seats was the provision of pneumatic assisted cushions to help them evacuate the aircraft in full flying gear in an emergency. (HSA Bitteswell)

other side of the City of Lincoln at Waddington where Nos. 44, 50, and 101 Sqdns were based with the Vulcan B.1A. With the change in the method of weapons delivery, so the aircraft of Bomber Command began to lose their gloss white anti-flash finish. This was replaced on the upper surfaces by a disruptive pattern of dark grey and medium green, the under surfaces retaining the original gloss white.

Flying at low level is not without its risks, thus some of the technical updates and modifications that were soon to arrive would be warmly welcomed. Possibly one of the most useful innovations was the introduction of the Terrain Following Radar housed in a small pod at the tip of the Vulcan's nose. Developed by Ferranti from the concept first put forward for a similar device in the innovative General Dynamics F-111, the TFR was first trialed on XM606 during 1966. Further improvements to other areas

of the avionics also took place later in this decade when the X-band jamming suite was fitted to the majority of the fleet. This device had first been tested in partial form using only one emitter head on XL388 and the BCDU allocated B.1A XA907. Later modified Vulcans gained two emitter heads, the trials aircraft retaining only the one throughout its service life until scrapped at RAF St.Athan. Intended mainly to counter the threat of detection by Soviet fighters the only visible presence of the system was a dome located on the forward ECM access door.

This decade not only saw the Vulcan receiving technical upgrades, operationally too there were great changes afoot. At 00.01 hours on Tuesday 30 April 1968, both Fighter Command and Bomber Command ceased to exist emerging as the unified Strike Command. In common with other organisations there was a reshuffle of available assets.

For the "V" force this meant that all the bomber and Victor tankers came under the control of No.1 (Bomber) Group headquartered at Bawtry, Yorkshire. An event of even greater significance took place in June 1969 when the baton of the primary nuclear deterrent was handed over to the Polaris submarine fleet of the Royal Navy. For the Vulcan this meant that all weapons had reverted to freefall delivery whether they be Strike (nuclear) or Attack (conventional). Changes in available weapons for use by the bomber had also taken place. For the strike role the WE.177 had become the prime nuclear shape, whilst for the conventional role the 1,000 lbs. retarded bomb had become part of the arsenal. This bomb allowed the Vulcan to carry out conventional low level attacks without the hazard of damage from its own weapons. Another change to the makeup of Strike Command had already taken place earlier when 35 Sqdn had been redeployed to Akrotiri on the Island of Cyprus in January 1969 where it was joined in February by 9 Sqdn. Both units had been deployed as an element of NEAF to the NATO southern flank as part of a strategy to counter the threat of perceived Soviet expansionism in the Mediterranean.

The change of owning command in the UK had also brought on the disappearance of QRA which had been causing morale problems amongst those involved and their families. It was replaced in turn by the far more relaxed "Edith Standby." This comprised of, normally, two aircraft in a squadron being re-roled from conventional attack to the strike attack role on a Friday. Although not including nuclear weapons in its setup (the process

stopped just short), the role change looked fairly simple on paper involving no more than a panel change at the Nav Rads position. However the functional checks afterwards could be time consuming and became even more so should the aircraft have a WRS (weapons release simulator) on board as well as 28 lbs. S&F (smoke and flash) bombs. Prior to derole after the weekend standby, the strike configured Vulcans would normally fly a simulated strike sortie that culminated in a bomb release over the Wainfleet range. The WRS would electronically simulate the release of a full-sized shape whilst the 28 lbs. S&F would indicate the position of impact to the range marshalls. Careful analysis afterwards would verify the accuracy of both aircraft and crew.

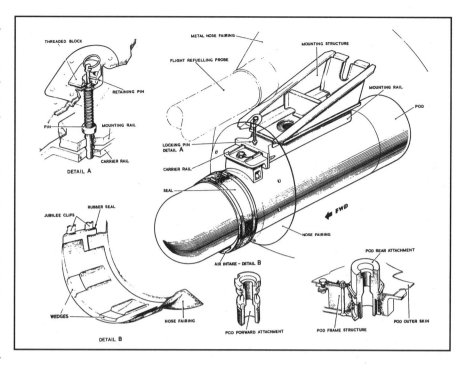

When the TFR installation programme began in 1967 the modifications required were minimal. Cut outs for clearance were required on the radome and a mounting rack was bolted to the metal nose beak. Surrounding the pod was a shroud which incorporated small ram air cooling intakes. (NATO AM)

Still wearing the fin badge of A&AEE, XM609, epitomises the standard that marked the Vulcan fleet in the late 1960s. The TFR pod is fitted as is a partial "X" band aerial installation. The next items that would undergo change would be the VHF aerials on the bomb aimer blister and the upper fuselage. (C. P. Russell-Smith Collection)

Circling Akrotiri after a roller landing the airbrakes of XH560 of the NEAF wing are retracting to the closed position. This angle emphasises the area of the Vulcan's wing very well. (John Nickolls)

As the Vulcans transitioned into the 1970s their dispersal was as follows. At Waddington Nos. 44, 50, and 101 Squadrons were operational whilst at Scampton Nos. 27 and 617 Squadron plus 230 OCU maintained their presence whilst on the strength of NEAF were the Vulcans of 9 and 35 Squadrons. The latter units operating in conjunction with the Lightnings of 56 Sqdn had been successful in discouraging Soviet adventures in the Middle East. However this changed almost overnight with the invasion of northern Cyprus in 1974 by the armed forces of Turkey. For safety's sake it was decided to remove the Vulcans from Akrotiri and return them to the UK. Thus the aircraft of 9 Sqdn were dispersed to Waddington whilst those of 35 Sqdn were sent to Scampton. Initially it had been intended to return the NEAF Bomber Wing to Cyprus after hostilities had ceased, however Britain was undergoing yet another period of economic uncertainty which was resulting in cutbacks in many Government provided services. Therefore the plan was scrapped and both units remained in the UK until disbandment.

As the Vulcan force entered the new decade a problem that had appeared on occasion reoccurred with some severity. In order to extend the aircraft's range and available training without being dependent on air refuelling a range of bomb bay fuel tanks had been developed. Initially these were of the saddle type for the Blue Steel role and contained 5,000 lbs. of fuel. Later for the conventional role the cylindrical or drum type had been developed and these were capable of holding up to 8,000 lbs. of fuel. Normal positioning within the bomb bay meant that they occupied the fore and aft slots, the centre remaining free for any other stores. Running along the edge of each bomb door was a collector gallery to which each tank was connected. All this extra fuel was thus vulnerable should a catastrophic engine failure occur.

Such an event duly happened on 8 January 1971 when Vulcan B.2 XM610 suffered a major failure of No.1 ECU. The ejected compressor blades also extensively damaged the next door No.2 engine. Such was the force of the resultant explosion that unbeknownst to the crew, part of the engine had entered the bomb bay and started a fuel fire to add to the one blazing in the port wing. This damage had been caused by red hot compressor blades penetrating the outer engine bay walls and entering the wing space and bomb bay. When the fire indicators finally showed on the warning panel, all the relevant fire extinguishers were operated and the stricken Vulcan turned towards the nearest RAF base at Leeming where the Captain intended to make an emergency landing. Although the extinguishers in both the wing and bomb bay had been fired, the strength of the conflagration was such as to overcome the methyl bromide extinguishant. Realising the seriousness of the situation the aircraft Captain ordered the crew to abandon the Vulcan whilst he turned the bomber towards the sea. Although the pilot stayed with the aircraft as long as possible, total loss of control when the runs finally burned through meant that he had to eject. All crew members escaped successfully –

the aircraft crashed near Wingate in County Durham without casualties.

The primary result of this accident and a similar incident later in the year was the reinforcement of the structure surrounding the engine bays plus an improvement to the containment shield on the Olympus engine itself. Improvements to the Vulcan's defensive electronics suite were also under scrutiny – the upshot of which was the appearance of XM597 in 1972 complete with squared off fin cap. This now housed a Marconi ARI 18228 passive warning receiver in place of the earlier Blue Saga jamming system as such detection was becoming the preferred modus operandi instead of the give away transmissions of the Red Steer TWR. Eventu-

ally all the in service Vulcan B.2 fleet underwent this modification, although for the first few years there were occasionally operating difficulties when "Green Butter" (ARI 18228) and Red Steer were online together. After much research by both Marconi and RAF avionics personnel, a form of shielding was devised that contained most of the effects although the problem was never completely eradicated.

From an engineer's point of view there are two reasons for aircraft modification, the first is due to the appearance of new or improved equipment, the second in occasionally tragic circumstances is caused by equipment failure which results in the destruction of an aircraft. In the case of the latter, the loss of

XM600 on 17 January 1977, without fatalities, near Spilsby, Lincolnshire, resulted in urgent fleet-wide modification action being required. The accident investigation branch were eventually able to conclude that the prime cause of destruction was that the wing fuel gallery running above the deployed RAT had sprung a minute leak. This had allowed fuel to drip onto the normally exposed live RAT cable connectors and vapourise. This in turn caused a fire and explosion which became uncontrollable, the crew finally abandoning aircraft when it was realised that reaching Waddington was out of the question. This potentially serious defect was further reinforced a few days later when XM597, also of 101 Sqdn, landed safely trailing smoke from the same

Sitting on its dispersal at Luqa, Malta, Vulcan B.2, XL318, of 27 Sqdn has its bomb doors open. This indicates that either the hydraulic system needs replenishing or that it is due to be loaded with ordnance. For ground purposes the normal method of opening the bomb bay doors was to use the EHPP although this frequently required that the normal and emergency reservoirs would need balancing afterwards. (C. P. Russell-Smith Collection)

Caught at a quiet moment is XJ823 of 50 Sqdn. The powerset plugged into the Vulcan was the normal state of affairs. When power was first applied it was 28v DC only there being a checklist of at least twenty items to be carried out before 200vAC was available. This was intended to cut out inadvertent accidents should some of the cockpit switches be in the wrong place. A giraffe stands at the intake indicating that either the engines were undergoing inspection or the intakes themselves required possible repair. Late in the life of the Vulcan fleet cracks began to appear in some of the intake panels necessitating repairs. (Mel James)

area. Rectification action was swift and involved in-depth inspection of the fuel gallery pipework and the provision of protective covering for the RAT cable connectors. The final cause was attributed to fatigue failure due to age.

A major change overtook a small portion of the Vulcan fleet on 1973 when the first Vulcan SR.2/B.2 MRR was rolled out. Covering no more than a handful of bombers the conversion programme was intended as a replacement for the dedicated Victor SR.2s of 543 Sqdn which were being withdrawn for conversion to K.2 tanker status. No. 27 Sqdn having disbanded from the bomber role in March 1972 reformed at Scampton on 1 November 1973 and worked up to operational status quickly which allowed 543 Sqdn to officially disband at Wyton on 24 May 1974. Typical tasks allocated to the squadron included overflying the many oil

Wearing the colours of 101 Sqdn XL360 is undergoing preparation for a ranger flight to Canada. Already any defective wheels have been replaced and the 4,000 lbs. pannier and beam awaits fitting in the bomb bay. Due to the size of this installation only a front fuel tank could be fitted. (Mel James)

Bereft of any form of unit marking B.2, XM609, rotates from the runway at Upper Heyford. This bomber had been one of the trials aircraft for the "X" band jamming system evidenced by the single emitter head under the forward access door. Production versions also had a forward facing emitter. (C. P. Russell-Smith Collection)

rigs in the North Sea, a duty shared with the Nimrod anti-submarine aircraft, on anti-terrorist patrol. Also on the list was a far more onerous and potentially hazardous duty, that of collecting upper atmosphere dust samples down range of nuclear test explosions. To accomplish this, two collection methods were employed known as Alpha and Omega. The primary "Alpha" collected its samples in under wingpods converted from Sea Vixen fuel tanks whilst the "Omega" required that some samples be collected by the aircraft flying through the dust cloud collecting samples via probes inserted into the airflow through the cockpit sextant mounts. Mainly for the purposes of this mission the Vulcans of 27 Sqdn retained a gloss finish in preference to the more prevalent matte as the former was far easier to clean of hot materials.

By the end of the decade the Vulcan fleet numbered eight squadrons with one OCU, but there was a replacement sitting in the wings to replace this still potent, but aged

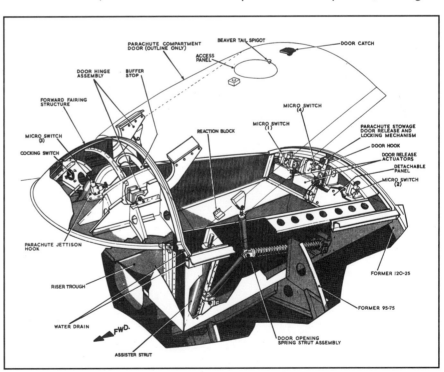

When first designed, the TBC door was wound shut using a special tool. After a series of fatal accidents the tool was replaced by a winch that made the whole process safer. (HSA Bitteswell)

Approaching for a landing the view of XJ823 reveals it to be a B.2 (MRR) although only the deletion of the TFR and the application of an overall gloss finish betrays its new role. (C. P. Russell-Smith Collection)

veteran – the Panavia Tornado. In 1981 No. 230 OCU, the Vulcan conversion school, disbanded being quickly followed by another Scampton unit 617 Sqdn. The following year saw the disappearance of Scampton's two other squadrons when 27 and 35 retired their aircraft; they were joined by the first of the Waddington units to go, No.9 Sqdn.

The final disappearance of the Vulcan from the RAF's Order of Battle was to be delayed by events in the South Atlantic. Needing a long range bomber the disbandment of the remaining Waddington squadrons was delayed as the old warhorse was prepared for its role in the countering of the Argentine invasion of the Falklands.

Vulcan B.2 XM612 of 101 Sqdn at RAF Waddington sits "locked and chocked" for the weekend. Intake and exhaust blanks are fitted to this series 301 ECU aircraft and judging by its stance it's fully fuelled for a Monday morning flight. Not visible in this shot, but fitted, is the tie-down hook which kept the Vulcan's nose firmly anchored to the ground in high winds. (Mel James)

VULCAN 7 AT WAR

THE FALKLANDS, CORPORATE, AND BEYOND

On 1 April 1982, the armed forces of Argentina invaded the Falkland Islands in the South Atlantic having occupied the islands of South Georgia a few days earlier. This was seen by many outsiders as an attempt by the Military Junta governing Argentina to deflect both internal and external criticism concerning the abuse of human rights and to deflect concern from the country's collapsing economy where inflation was running rampant.

Eight thousand miles away in London there was speculation before and after the invasion that the F&CO of the British Government had a strong suspicion that such events were about to take place and had for domestic political reasons decided to play it low key. Whatever the reasons, the Governor of the Islands, Mr. Rex Hunt, decided to surrender to the invaders in order to protect the civilian population and the small token force of Royal Marines stationed in Port Stanley, the capital.

Once the government of Mrs. Thatcher had decided to act, it was obvious from the outset that the recovery of the Falklands would be a logistical nightmare. However a solution to part of the problem was soon found in the shape of Ascension Island, a British Protectorate. Amongst all the tabloid jingoism of departures a base had been found to act as a jumping off point complete with an airfield at Wideawake Airport. To and from here supplies and aircraft began to flow all head-

ing south. Command strategic planners had realised very early in the campaign that airpower would be the key to success. Much of the air support required to recapture the islands would be provided by the Harriers and Sea Harriers of the RAF and Royal Navy respectively although other types would undoubtedly be needed.

However both variants of this intriguing V/STOL aircraft were intended for CAP and close air support attack duties, and their use in the subsequent fighting was felt to carry very little in the way of strategic impact.

Whilst the turmoil of the invasion had been taking place the Vulcan fleet of Strike Command was close

to finishing service. Already the three Scampton units Nos. 27, 35, and 617 Sqdns had disappeared, whilst over at Waddington No. 9 Sqdn was already in the process of transitioning to the Tornado. This left 44, 50, and 101 Squadrons still active with the Vulcan B.2 at this Lincolnshire base. Of all the aircraft in the active inventory, the Vulcan was the only long range attack aircraft capable of conveying a large quantity of bombs and other weapons to targets on the Falkland Islands and any other designated targets. One deficiency that was immediately apparent was that of range. Although all in service aircraft were equipped to carry bomb bay fuel tanks, it was felt that 16,000 lbs. of extra fuel would not be enough to reach a target, drop

With the volcanic hills of Ascension Island as a backdrop, Vulcan XM607 returns to its parking slot at Wideawake complete with ECM pod under the starboard wing. Behind the Vulcan are Nimrod anti-submarine aircraft whilst to the left a Victor tanker is visible. (Mel James)

the required weapons and return safely. The fitment of the overload tanks also reduced the available offensive load considerably to a third of its maximum. This too was regarded as unacceptable and would be seen worldwide as an inefficient use of such an asset. The answer of course was to re-instate the long dormant in-flight refuelling system which caused a monumental amount of work to restore.

Arriving at the target safely was only the first step in an attack as there would be the obstacle of the Argentine AAA and SAM guidance radars to overcome. Here too the Vulcan was to play a vital role in suppressing and attacking the Argentine defensive assets. Even Vulcans scheduled for scrapping played a vital role by supplying their refuel probes to other aircraft of the RAF such as the Nimrod and Hercules. To adapt the bomber to carry external weapons for the

SEAD role, those aircraft that still had their built-in wing Skybolt mounts intact plus, more importantly, the cabling required were chosen from the survivors to deploy south. Although some pylons had been manufactured for the Skybolt compatibility programme, none remained extant. Therefore the engineers at Waddington, led by Squadron Leaders Chris Pye and Mel James, set about creating their own. Based upon a length of steel joist with mounting shackles this engineering innovation was soon tidied up by the addition of the necessary cable looms, fairings, and weapons mounts. The first weapon chosen for the SEAD role was one that the RAF had plenty of – the Martel air-to-ground missile which came in TV-steered or radar-guided form. Complete with the new pylons, XM597 carried out four live firings of the missile over Aberporth range during 4/5 May 1982.

However there were other perceived calls upon the services of such a versatile weapon and it was soon re-allocated to the Nimrod anti-submarine fleet. In its place the United States offered the AGM-45 Shrike anti-radar missile. Test firings of this new weapon to the RAF were soon arranged as all modifications were taking place within days, not the normal weeks that such processes usually took. The realisation that pylon-mounted external stores had little or no effect upon the Vulcans aerodynamic handling led to further trials being carried out.

Although never used in anger, at least one Vulcan was used to investigate the possibility of fitting underwing fuel tanks in an effort to improve range and reduce the number of support tankers required to get the bomber to its target. The chosen machine was XL387 that was standing on the scrapline at St Athan. External fuel tanks from a number of types including many that had long gone out of service were offered up to the airframe to check clearances especially in the vicinity of the main gear door. The selected fuel tank was the large overload specimen from the Hawker Hunter fighter. Connection of the tank to the main system would have meant some unsightly pipework coupled to the wing defuel points just outboard of the main gear bays. Two main reasons were offered in support of these trials. The first being that an inordinate number of Victor K.2 tankers were being used to launch and recover each mission thus depriving other users of this vital resource, the second was a look forward well into the future where the Vulcan would have been used to attack targets on the Argentine mainland should the sit-

Complete with the required solicitous messages, a clutch of 1,000 lbs. bombs is prepared for loading into the bomb bay. The Vulcan had three positions for mounting conventional weapons, each beam being capable of holding seven iron bombs. The release lanyards from the beam to each weapon can clearly be seen. (Mel James)

uation demand it. The extra few thousand pounds of fuel would have been enough to extend the bombers' range using the same amount of tankers. However as events unfolded the requirement for Vulcan strikes against the mainland faded and the idea was shelved. The test airframe, once poised for a return to service, was later scrapped. The same future contingency planning that had been investigating the external fuel tank idea also recommended that the scrapping policy be put on hold and that the personnel from the St. Athan major servicing team were placed on standby for servicing of the Vulcans to resume.

The final irony that caps the events in the South Atlantic was that a delegation from the Fuerza Aerea Argentina had visited the UK early in 1982 to discuss purchase of a quantity of redundant Vulcans plus a substantial spares package. In light of the invasion of the Falklands, the possible sale of redundant members of the Vulcan fleet to Argentina was hastily dropped. Instead the in service aircraft at Waddington were prepared for their only foray into war. A total of ten aircraft were selected from the survivors as they retained all the required Skybolt fitments. From this total a final six were designated for modification and deployment. To man the aircraft, five crews were selected all of whom had recently taken part in the February 1982 Red Flag exercises in the United States. Two crews came from 50 Sqdn whilst 44 and 101 Sqdns provided one each. The final bomber crew came from the ranks of the recently disbanded 9 Sqdn. Further whittling amongst the Vulcans reduced the primaries to five in number, these being declared as available for "Operation Corporate." Training for missions began immediately with bombing and AAR being high on the agenda. The latter exercise being carried out at Marham during 14-17 April.

Further modifications were also being proposed to improve the Vulcan's chances. The first to be incorporated was the Carousel INS manufactured by DELCO as fitted to British Airways Boeing 747s. This modification was first flown in XM597, the rest of the five following shortly thereafter. Although the Vulcan was fitted with powerful ECM jamming equipment its prime

Standing on the second bomb beam an armourer connects up the various connectors of the weapons in slot one. The jack shown fully extended sits under a cut out in the beam and is attached to the aircraft by a hanging point. Once the beam is raised and locked the jack is disconnected and removed. (Mel James)

Improvisation is a key part in any successful military campaign. Here a Royal Air Force engineer prepares an ECM pod for loading onto the wing pylon of a Vulcan at Wideawake from a very makeshift trolley. (Mel James)

role was aimed at Soviet style radar systems. It was also fixed in nature and thus not retunable to different frequencies. This initially posed a problem as the equipment supplied to the Argentine armed forces was of western origin and could not be deceived by the on board systems fitted to the Vulcan. The answer was to fit the necessary cabling and panels to operate a Westinghouse AN/ALQ-101 jamming pod which was then carried on the starboard wing pylon.

Trained, modified, and repainted the first two Vulcans, XM598 and XM607, and crews departed Waddington on the morning of 29 April for Ascension Island. A third aircraft, XM597, was launched as an airborne spare, but was not required and returned to base.

After two air-to-air refuellings from Victor tankers, the two aircraft landed at Wideawake later that day. The codename applied to the Vulcan missions was Black Buck, the first of which was launched during the night of 30 April/1 May. To support the primary and secondary aircraft, a fleet of eleven Victor tankers were deployed, the two Vulcans departing late in the sequence. The primary mission aircraft was designated as XM598 with XM607 acting as the airborne spare. In the event, the primary had to return to base as the captain's direct vision window would not seal properly, thus XM607 became the first Vulcan to drop bombs in anger.

Some two hours later, the Vulcan climbed to 10,000 ft. to begin the bombing run diagonally across the airfield at Stanley. With the bomb doors open and the bombing computer set for automatic cyclic release, the aircraft carried out its run across the target with all twenty-one bombs clearing the aircraft without problems. Virtually unchallenged, a SkyGuard radar did paint the Vulcan, but was immediately jammed, the bomber turned north and headed for Ascension.

Two important messages were delivered to Argentina as a result of the attack. The first was to show that any target within the Argentine sphere of influence could be attacked and the second confirmed that any diplomatic efforts to resolve the crisis were at an end. Black Buck two was launched on 3 May using XM607 as the primary. Yet again the airfield at Stanley was bombed successfully, the bomber returning to Ascension without incident. A third bombing mission (Black Buck 3) planned for 16 May was in the eventuality cancelled, both the deployed aircraft returning to Waddington instead.

Having shown the Junta ruling Argentina that bombing raids were possible any time and any place, thoughts turned to using the Vulcan in the other role envisaged for it, that of SEAD.

The one area that the Argentine forces had covered well was air defence and the radar network required to support it. This would obviously pose a threat when the time came to use the Harriers and Sea Harriers in the ground attack role. To counter the radar threat trials were carried out using a Vulcan, XM594, equipped with Martel AS.37 missiles. Although successful it was decided to accept the American offer of AGM-45 Shrike ARMs

instead. This involved loading up to four Shrikes per aircraft, trials of this configuration were acceptable although the normal load was to be two missiles loaded on the port pylon only. Two of the Black Buck aircraft were chosen to act as carriers these being XM597, primary, and XM598 as secondary.

Deployment of the two Shrike equipped aircraft began on Ascension on 26 May. The first mission (Black Buck 4) was launched at midnight 28 May using XM597 as the primary. Unfortunately the aircraft had to return to base some five hours later when the HDU of the lead Victor failed. A further radar hunting mission (Black Buck 5) was launched on 30 May just before midnight. This time the transit passed without problems and the Vulcan and its crew settled down to a period of watching and waiting. Only one air defence radar came on line and it was promptly fired at. The first missile locked on, but missed the target and exploded some yards away causing only minor damage to the array. The second lost the lock-on completely after launch and crashed quite a distance away from the intended target.

Radar hunting and destruction was also the purpose of Black Buck 6 launched in the late evening of 2 June. The primary aircraft was again XM597 this time loaded with four Shrike missiles. Again the bomber reached the Falklands without incident and began its loiter above the Islands waiting for a transmitter to switch on. Realising that the enemy might need some encouragement, the crew of the Vulcan began a dummy descent towards the airfield. This had the desired effect as a fire control radar in the vicinity of Port Stanley came on line and

Awaiting their next sortie are Vulcans XM598 and XM607 at Wideawake airfield. By this time both aircraft had INS fitted, underwing pylons, and a reinstated flight refuelling system. (Mel James)

began to track the bomber. Two Shrikes were promptly launched at this target completely destroying it.

Although the mission was successful the Vulcan was at the end of its allotted loiter period and thus turned for Ascension. An on-time, on-track rendezvous with a waiting Victor was made and AAR began. However during the refuel the Vulcan probe tip broke off effectively ending fuel transfer. The

nearest diversion airfield was Rio in Brazil and course was set in that direction. As the on board fuel state was low, the Vulcan was climbed to its economical cruise height of 40,000 ft. As two Shrikes still remained on the aircraft, attempts were made to fire them off. The first cleared the aircraft properly, the second hung up despite all attempts to shake it free. As a further precaution, all classified documents were gathered together in a

This Vulcan is the famous XM597 whose emergency diversion to Brazil after refuel probe problems is celebrated by the Brazilian flag. Also visible are two Shrike symbols. (Damien Burke)

Coming close to the end of its service career, XM650 once on the strength of 101 Sqdn reveals the final standard of the Vulcan in its last days. The "L" band aerial has been removed although the "X" band still remains. By this time the aircraft was with 50 Sqdn and was to lose its probe to another type before long. (Mel James)

holdall and launched through the crew entrance door, the crew having donned their masks for 100% oxygen before depressurising the cabin. Inbound to Rio the Vulcans crew were evasive about their identity as hurried diplomatic efforts were being made to give landing clearance. The frantic efforts of the British diplomats paid off as permission was finally granted by Rio de Janerio Air Traffic Control. As the approach was commenced, a fighter escort courtesy of the FAB arrived to shepherd the Vulcan to the airport. After an immaculate landing the aircraft was taxied to a parking slot and the engines shut down. At this point a total of 2,000 lbs. of usable fuel remained in the tanks, enough only for a few minutes of flying. Both the aircraft and the hung-up Shrike were impounded by the Brazilian authorities

although the Vulcan was later released and flown to Wideawake on 10 June. On Ascension, a replacement probe was fitted and the Vulcan returned home to Waddington on 13 June.

A final Black Buck mission, number 7, was mounted on 11 June using XM607 as the primary aircraft. Similar in execution to Black Buck 1, the bombing run across Stanley airfield met with no resistance and the aircraft returned to base without incident. On 14 June 1982, Vulcans XM598 and XM607 were flown home to Waddington. The Argentine forces surrendered on that day – for the Vulcan and its crews, the aircraft's only period of war service was now complete.

Although the Vulcan as a pure bomber was to fade from the RAF

inventory very quickly after Operation Corporate, a handful were to linger on in a previously unforeseen role. During the conflict the fatigue lives of the Victor tankers had been consumed at a higher than planned rate. Replacement in the form of converted ex-civil Vickers VC-10s and Lockheed L-1011 Tristars was already being planned. However a short term stopgap tanker was desperately required and the Vulcan seemed to be the ideal answer.

With a basic fuel load of 72,400 lbs., the addition of 24,000 lbs. in three bomb bay tanks gave a reasonable amount of disposable fuel. Initial studies by BAe and Waddington engineering staff had shown that it was possible to fit a dispensing HDU into the ECM tailcone, albeit that it would have to be split to fit it all in. Centreline HDUs were drawn from stocks put aside for the VC-10 tanker conversion programme as it was estimated that it would be at least two years before the converted airliners could accept the missing equipment. Six Vulcans were therefore selected for conversion, these being XH558, XH560, XH561, XJ825, XL445, and XM571. All were sent to the BAe factory at Woodford for conversion. Upon arrival the redundant ECM systems were stripped out, their place being taken by the HDU. Extra pipework was then fed through the old Blue Steel rear fuselage fairing into the bomb bay where it was coupled up to extensions made to the already installed fuel galleries. The section of the HDU that intruded into the airflow was housed in a tapered box structure that also featured banks of refuel lights fitted to each outer sidewall. The displaced tail bumper was replaced by a longer sprung arm located below the HDU box.

The first flight of a Vulcan K.2 conversion was undertaken by XH561 on 18 June. All six aircraft were returned to 50 Sqdn at Waddington between August and November 1982 where they operated in concert with four standard B.2s retained for training purposes. On 31 March 1984, No.50 Sqdn RAF finally relinquished its Vulcan K.2s having flown some 3,000 hours in the tanker support role. The frontline career of this fine aircraft had finally come to an end.

In addition to the conversion work undertaken at Woodford, the opportunity was taken to carry out some routine maintenance. The unidentified B.2 behind XH561 is surrounded by aircraft components, access stands, and tool kits. (BAe/Avro Heritage)

On 13 July 1982 K.2 XM571 was photographed undertaking its preservice release trials. The various markings on the hose indicate to dispenser and receiver whether the hose is in such a position to dispense fuel as the hose has to reach a certain length to open the valves. (BAe/Avro Heritage)

"Now is not the time to wonder if it will fit." Staff at Woodford discuss the final details prior to installing the drogue part of the HDU into the aircraft. The drives and associated components are already in position. (BAe/Avro Heritage)

The first HDU is carefully loaded into the rear fuselage that once housed the bomber's ECM. The vehicle in use is a missile loader. Although unidentified, the aircraft is possibly XH558 as it still has the underwing MRR sample pod fit. (BAe/Avro Heritage)

WARBIRDTECH
SERIES

Vulcan K.2 XH560 air refuels B.2 XL426 high above the Irish sea. The latter aircraft had been involved in the trials to clear the tanker for the refuel of "heavy" aircraft types. (BAe/Avro Heritage)

The structure of the HDU box was a mixture of wood, for the frangible parts, and aluminum for the main structure. Clearly visible here are the refuel control lights in their fairings. (Mel James)

The forward face of the HDU box reveals another cluster of lights. These were intended to light up the underside of the tanker in night conditions. (Mel James)

Awaiting its tug and handling party is XL427. Normally five people were required for a Vulcan movement although more could be provided for awkward situations. On a night move the AAPP was run to provide external lighting. (Mel James)

Once Operation Corporate was complete the scrapping of the Vulcan fleet resumed in earnest. Still wearing the colours of 35 Sqdn, XJ783 is undergoing spares reclamation. In the foreground stands a jet pipe end cap and the chutes that were once fitted to the window dispenser units located behind the main gear bays. (Mel James)

Vulcan K.2 XJ825 captured on display to the public. The addition of the HDU marred the lines of the Vulcan. When the HDU was fitted the Red Steer was replaced by a blank radome and the heat exchanger unit was removed from the rear fuselage. The outline of its fairing can quite clearly be seen on the paintwork. (C. P. Russell-Smith Collection)

THE VULCAN ALPHABET

AAA	Anti Aircraft Artillery		JATO	Jet Assisted Take Off
A&AEE	Aircraft and Armament Experimental Establishment		lbs. st.	pounds static thrust
AAPP	Airborne Auxiliary Power Pack			
AAR	Air to Air Refuelling		MoS	Ministry of Supply
ACM	Air Chief Marshall			
AEO	Air Electronics Operator		NATO	North Atlantic Treaty Organisation
AGL	Above Ground Level		NBS	Navigation Bombing System
AGM	Air to Ground Missile		NCO	Non Commissioned Officer
ALBM	Air Launched Ballistic Missile		NEAF	Near East Air Force
AN/ALQ	American Avionics Designation		NORAD	North American Air Defence
ARI	Air Radio/Radar Installation			
AW	Armstrong Whitworth		OCU	Operational Conversion Unit
			OR/OR BRANCH	Operation Requirement/Branch
B.2 (BS)	Vulcan B.2 (Blue Steel)		ORP	Operational Readiness Platform
B.2 MRR/SR.2	Vulcan B.2 Maritime Radar Reconnaissance/Strategic Reconnaissance			
			PFCU	Powered Flying Control Unit
BAe	British Aerospace		psi	pounds per square inch (Imperial)
BCBS/SCBS	Bomber Command Bombing School, later Strike Command			
			QRA	Quick Reaction Alert
BLEU	Blind Landing Experimental Unit			
BNS	Bombing Navigation System		RAE	Royal Aircraft Establishment
			RAF	Royal Air Force
C(A)	Controller (Aircraft)		RAT	Ram Air Turbine
C-IN-C	Commander in Chief			
CSDU	Constant Speed Drive Unit		SAC	Strategic Air Command
			SAM	Surface to Air Missile
ECM	Electronic Counter Measures		SBAC	Society of British Aircraft Constructors
ECU	Engine Change Unit		SEAD	Suppression of Enemy Air Defences
EE Co.	English Electric Company		SFOM	French optical sight manufacturer
EHPP	Emergency Hydraulic Power Pack		S&F	Smoke & Flash
FAB	*Forca Aerea Brasiliera*		TBC	Tail Brake Chute
F&CO	Foreign and Commonwealth Office		TFR	Terrain Following Radar
FSD	Full Scale Development		TNT	Tri-Nitro Toluene
FTS	Flying Training School		TRE	Telecommunications Research Establishment
H2S	Radar known as "Home Sweet Home"		TRU	Transformer Rectifier Unit
HDU	Hose Drogue Unit pronounced "Hoo Doo"		TSR	Tactical Strike Reconnaissance
			TWR	Tail Warning Radar
HP	Handley Page			
HTP	High Test Peroxide (oxidizer)		VCCP	Vapour Cycle Cooling Pack
			V/STOL	Vertical/Short Takeoff and Landing
ICBM	Inter Continental Ballistic Missile			
INS	Inertial Navigation System		WRS	Weapons Release Simulator

SIGNIFICANT DATES

1941
Maud Committee report on nuclear weapons released.

1942
Atomic bomb program ("Manhattan Project") formed in United States. Los Alamos, New Mexico.

16 July 1945
Trinity device exploded.

August 1945
Atomic weapons dropped on Hiroshima and Nagasaki.

October 1945
Atomic Energy Research Establishment created at Harwell, Oxon.

August 1946
McMahon Act passed – restricts passage of nuclear information to other countries.

17 December 1946
OR.229 released for Lancaster/Lincoln replacement.

1947
Defence Policy Steering Group outlines "Ten Year Plan" for development of weapon and aircraft.

28 July 1947
Tenders from AVRO and Handley Page accepted by MoS.

7 January 1947
Spec. B35/46 issued for new jet powered bomber.

August 1947
Shorts given ITP on Spec.B14/46 for SA.4 Sperrin.

1947
NATO formed.

1 January 1948
ITP issued to AVRO for quantity Type 698.

June 1948
Spec.E15/48 issued to AVRO for Type 707 and 710 research aircraft.

September 1948
Type 710 cancelled.

August 1949
First Type 707 completed. VX784 first flight 4 September.

6 May 1950
First ground run of Bristol BE.10 Olympus ECU.

August 1950
First flight of Type 707A VX790 research aircraft.

August 1951
Short SA.4 Sperrin flies. Programme cancelled soon after.

August 1952
Prototype 698 VX770 rolled out at Woodford, first flight 30 August.

14 August 1952
Contract 6/Acft/8442/CB.6(a) issued for 25 Vulcan B.1: XA889 to XA913.

3 October 1952
First UK nuclear device exploded. Codenamed "Hurricane."

May 1953
A.W. Sapphire engines fitted to VX770 in place of Avons.

3 May 1953
First flight of second prototype 698 VX777.

1954
Blue Steel development begins. Spec. 1132 issued to cover development.

27 July 1954
VX777 damaged in heavy landing.

30 September 1954
Second production order for 37 aircraft issued. Contract 6/Acft/11301/CB.6(a) XH475 to XH483, XH497 to XH506, XH532. Contract later split to 20 Vulcan B.1; 17 Vulcan B.2.

January 1955
First production Vulcan B.1 XA889 rolled out.

March 1955
Last 17 aircraft on final B.1 contract re-ordered as Vulcan B.2: XH533 to XH539, XH554 to XH563.

31 March 1955
Second Vulcan production order, 8 aircraft. Contract 6/Acft/11830/CB.6(a) XJ780 to XJ784, XJ823 to XJ825.

1956
Blue Danube enters service.

25 February 1956
Third production order for 24 Vulcan B.2 issued. Contract 6/Acft/13145/CB.6(a) XL317 to XL321, XL359 to XL36, XL384 to XL392, XL425 to XL427, XL443 to XL446.

March 1956
Spec.1159 to AVRO for Blue Steel second phase development.

29 May 1956
Vulcan B.1 cleared for operational RAF service.

August 1956
230 OCU formed to train Vulcan crews.

1 October 1956
First in service crash of Vulcan B.1 XA897 at Heathrow Airport.

July 1957
No. 83 Sqdn forms to operate Vulcan B.1.

31 August 1957
First flight of VX777 with Phase 2C wing intended for Vulcan B.2.

15 October 1957
No. 101 Sqdn reforms with Vulcan B.1.

Late 1957
First test drops of 2/3rd scale Blue Steel using Valliant B.1.

22 January 1958
Final production order for Vulcan B.2 issued for 40 aircraft: Contract KD/B/01/CB.6(A) XM569 to XM576, XM594 to XM612, and XM645 to XM657.

1 May 1958
No.617 Sqdn reforms with Vulcan B.1.

19 August 1958
First flight of XH533, the first production Vulcan B.2.

20 September 1958
Prototype VX770 destroyed after wing explosion overflying Syerston, Notts.

1959 to 1961
Trials of FSD Blue Steel at Woomera Range, Australia.

March 1960
Agreement to proceed with Skybolt air-launched ballistic missile programme concluded between U.S. and U.K.

May 1960
Vulcan B.2 cleared for operational RAF service.

July 1960
Conversion programme for Vulcan B.1 to B.1A begins.

August 1960
No.44 Sdqn forms with Vulcan B.1A.

10 October 1960
No.83 Sqdn re-equips with Vulcan B.2.

1 April 1961
No. 27 Sqdn forms with Vulcan B.2.

26 June 1961
No.101 Sqdn to Waddington with Vulcan B.1.

1 August 1961
No.50 Sqdn receives Vulcan B.1A.

1 September 1961
No. 617 Sqdn re-equips with Vulcan B.2.

December 1961
Test drops of dummy Skybolt carried out by Vulcan B.2s.

1 March 1962
No.9 Sqdn receives Vulcan B.2.

12 July 1962
No.12 Sqdn equips with Vulcan B.2.

September 1962
Blue Steel enters service with 617 Sqdn.

November 1962
Skybolt programme cancelled.

6 March 1963
Final Vulcan B.1A conversion re-enters service.

December 1964
Last Vulcan B.2 XM657 delivered to Bomber Command.

1966
First trials of TFR using XM606.

1966 to 1967
Vulcan B.1/ B.1A withdrawals.

30 April 1968
Strike Command formed from Bomber and Fighter Commands.

February/March 1969
Nos.9 and 35 Sqdns form NEAF Bomber Wing, Cyprus.

30 June 1969
Nuclear deterrent role handed over from Blue Steel to RN Polaris.

June 1972
Trials begin with ARI18228 fitted to XM597.

1 November 1973
No.27 Sqdn re-equips with Vulcan SR.2/B2 (MRR).

Early 1974
Nos. 9 and 35 Sqdns return to UK permanently after invasion of Cyprus by Turkish forces.

1981
230 OCU disbands.

31 December 1981
No.617 Sqdn disbands as Vulcan unit.

1 March 1982
No.35 Sqdn disbands.

30 March 1982
27 Sqdn disbands.

1 April 1982
Argentine forces occupy Falkland Islands.

April 1982
Vulcan units begin preparation for Operation Corporate.

29 April 1982
First two Vulcans deploy to Ascension Island.

30 April 1982
First Vulcan to Woodford for conversion to K.2 tanker.

30 April/1 May 1982
Black Buck 1 bombing raid on the Falklands launched.

1 May 1982
No.9 Sqdn officially disbands.

3 May 1982
Black Buck 2 bombing raid undertaken.

4/5 May 1982
Test firings of Martel Missiles carried out from external pylons.

16 May 1982
Black Buck 3 cancelled.

28 May 1982
Black Buck 4 launched.

30 May 1982
Black Buck 5 launched.

2 June 1982
Black Buck 6 launched.

11 June 1982
Black Buck 7 launched.

14 June 1982
Vulcans return to Waddington. Argentine forces on the Falkland Islands surrender.

18 June 1982
First flight of Vulcan K.2 tanker.

23 June 1982
C(A) release for K.2 granted. Deliveries to 50 Sqdn.

4 August 1982
No.101 Sqdn disbands.

21 December 1982
No.44 Sqdn disbands.

31 March 1984
No.50 Sqdn disbands. Vulcan leaves RAF service.

After retirement some Vulcans were lucky enough to be selected for preservation. One of these is B.2 XM655 once of 101 Sqdn (as was the author!) although it carries 50 Sqdn marks here. Substantially complete, the bomber does lack much of its classified avionics equipment and its flight refuelling probe which, like many others, was removed for use on other types. (Damien Burke)